bikeline®-Danube Bike Trail 1
© 2008-2014, **Verlag Esterbauer GmbH**
A-3751 Rodingersdorf, Hauptstr. 31
Tel.: +43/2983/28982-0, Fax: -500
E-Mail: bikeline@esterbauer.com
www.esterbauer.com
3rd edition 2014
ISBN: 978-3-85000-617-0

Please quote edition and ISBN number in all correspondence!

We are especially grateful to Ms. Kathy Kist of Cincinnati, whose generous support made the translation of this book possible.
We wish to thank all the people who contributed to the production of this book, see p. 153

The bikeline-Team: Birgit Albrecht-Walzer, Heidi Authried, Beatrix Bauer, Markus Belz, Michael Bernhard, Michael Binder, Veronika Bock, Petra Bruckmüller, Sandra Eisner, Roland Esterbauer, Dagmar Güldenpfennig, Tobias Klein, Martina Kreindl, Nora Ludolph, Bettina Müllauer, Eveline Müllauer, Gregor Münch, Karin Neichsner, Niki Nowak, Carmen Paradeiser, Julia Pelikan, Christian Schlechte, Erik Schmidt, Martina Specht, Matthias Thal, Martin Trippmacher, Martin Wischin, Wolfgang Zangerl

2

Cover photos: Schloss Grünau, by Weltenburg, Regensburg: Gaby Sipöcz;
Photo credits: Archiv: 44, 49, 50, 63, 132; Birgit Albrecht-Walzer: 79; Baden-Württemberg Tourismus-Marketing: 60; Bürgermeisteramt Inzigkofen: 30, 31; Fremdenverkehrsverein /Tourist-Information Donauwörth: 80; FVV Ostbayern: 122, 130; Gahr & Popp Fotowerkstatt: 118; Gemeinde Immendingen: 22; Gemeinde Obermarchtal: 42; Gemeindeverwaltungsverband Donau-Heuberg: 27; Gaby Sipöcz: 20, 28, 92, 94, 100, 134; Hundersingen: 36; Ingolstadt Tourismus und Kongress GmbH, Tanja Lehner: 88; Landkreis Regensburg: 114; Passau Tourismus e.V.: 136; Roland Esterbauer: 22, 27; Regensburg Tourismus GmbH: 106, 108, 110; Schloss Kalteneck: 78; Stadt Donaueschingen: 18; Stadt Ehingen: 48; Stadt Gundelfingen: 70; Stadt Günzburg: 68; Stadt Kelheim: 98, 100; Stadt Kelheim, Verena Lindner: 103; Stadt Mühlheim an der Donau: 26; Stadt Neuburg a. d. Donau: 84, 86; Stadt Tuttlingen: 23; Stadtverwaltung Dillingen: 71; Stadtverwaltung Mengen: 34, 36; Stadtverwaltung Riedlingen: 41; TI Sigmaringen, Achim Mende: 32; Tourismus-Marketing GmbH Baden-Württemberg/TMBW: 58; Verkehrsamt Höchstädt an der Donau: 74, 76

GPS-Track Download

The GPS tracks for this book is available after registration on the internet:
www.esterbauer.com

Produktcode: 617-7745-A3D6

What is bikeline?

We are a team of writers, cartographers, geographers and other staff united by our enthusiasm for bicycling and touring. Our project first „got rolling" in 1987, when a group of Vienna cyclists came together to begin producing bicycling maps. Today we are a highly successful publisher that offers a wide range of bikeline® and cycline® books in five languages covering many European countries.

We need your help to keep our books up-to-date. Please write to us if you find errors or changes. We would also be grateful for experiences and impressions from your own cycling tours.

We look forward to your letters and e-mails (redaktion@esterbauer.com),

Your bikeline team

Preface

From its headwaters in the Black Forest of southwestern Germany, the Danube flows through some of the most beautiful landscapes in Europe. Pristine flood-plains, picturesque villages and small towns, and a wealth of cultural landmarks line the river as it begins its long march to the distant Black Sea.

These tranquil valleys are also ideal for cycling. In recent years, many of the paths and lanes along the river have been paved specifically for bicycle tourists. As a result, almost the entire route follows smooth quiet roads that make it ideal for families with children.

Precise maps, reliable route descriptions, information about historic and cultural attractions plus a comprehensive list of overnight accommodation – this book provides everything you need for a cycling tour along the German Danube. The one thing it cannot provide is great cycling weather, but we hope you encounter nothing but sunshine and gentle tailwinds.

Map legend

Cycling routes (Radrouten)

Main cycle route, low motor traffic
(Hauptroute, wenig KFZ-Verkehr)

———— Paved surface (asphaltiert)
– – – – Unpaved surface (nicht asphaltiert)
▪▪▪▪▪▪ Bad surface (schlecht befahrbar)

Main cycle route, without motor traffic / cycle path
(Hauptroute, autofrei / Radweg)

———— Paved surface (asphaltiert)
▬ ▬ ▬ Unpaved surface (nicht asphaltiert)
▪▪▪▪▪▪▪ Bad surface (schlecht befahrbar)

Excursion or alternative cycle route, low motor traffic
(Ausflug od. Variante, wenig KFZ-Verkehr)

———— Paved surface (asphaltiert)
– – – Unpaved surface (nicht asphaltiert)
▪▪▪▪▪ Bad surface (schlecht befahrbar)

Excursion or alternative route, without motor traffic / cycle path (Ausflug od. Variante, autofrei / Radweg)

———— Paved surface (asphaltiert)
▬ ▬ ▬ Unpaved surface (nicht asphaltiert)
▪▪▪▪▪▪▪ Bad surface (schlecht befahrbar)

Other cycle routes (Sonstiges)

———— Other cycle route (sonstige Radroute)

---

ooooooo Planned cycle path (Radweg in Planung)
xxxxxxx Closed cycle path (Radweg gesperrt)
ıııııııııı Dismounting recommended (Schiebestrecke)
━━━━━━ One-way connection (Einbahnführung)
━╤━╤━ Train connection (Zugverbindung)
⊶⊷⊶ Ferry connection (Fährverbindung)
ıııııııııııı Cobbled street (Kopfsteinpflaster)
═══════ Tunnel (Tunnel)
● ● ● ● ● ● Cycle route with significant motor traffic (verkehrsreiche Radroute)
▦▦▦▦▦▦ Cycle lane (Radfahrstreifen)
━━━━━━ Cycle path along road (straßenbegleitender Radweg)
x x x x Road closed to cyclists (Straße für Radfahrer gesperrt)

⇨ Described direction (Beschriebene Fahrtrichtung)
⑤ Waypoint (Wegpunkt)

Gradient / distance (Steigungen / Entfernungen)

➤ Steep gradient, uphill (starke Steigung)
➤ Light gradient, uphill (leichte bis mittlere Steigung)
╲2,4╱ Distance in km (Entfernung in Kilometern)
The values may differ from actual distances due to rounding off. (Durch Rundungen können Differenzen zu den tatsächlich gefahrenen Kilometern entstehen.)

Important cycling information (Radinformationen)

🔧 Bike workshop* (Fahrradwerkstatt*)
🚲 Bike rental* (Fahrradvermietung*)
🚲 Covered bike stands* (überdachter Abstellplatz*)
🚲 Lockable bike stands* (abschließbarer Abstellplatz*)
🔌 E-bike charging station (E-bike Ladestation)
ℹ Information board* (Infotafel*)
⚠ Dangerous section (Gefahrenstelle)
⚠ Read text carefully (Text beachten)
🪜 Stairs (Treppe)
🚲 Bicycle must be carried! (Tragestrecke)
≍ Constriction, bottleneck* (Engstelle*)

⬚ Town or city map (Stadt- /Ortsplan)

Symbols only in the city maps (Nur in Ortsplänen)

🅿 Garage* (Parkhaus*)
🎭 Theatre* (theater*)
✉ Post office* (Post*)
💊 Pharmacy* (Apotheke*)
🄷 Hospital* (Krankenhaus*)
🄵 Fire brigade* (Feuerwehr*)
🅄 Police* (Polizei*)

* **Selection** (* Auswahl)

Scale 1 : 50.000

1 cm ≙ 500 m   1 km ≙ 2 cm

4

0   1   2   3   4   5   6   7   8   9   10 km

Sights of interest / Facilities (Sehenswertes / Einrichtungen)

- Church; Chapel (Kirche; Kapelle)
- Monastery/Convent (Kloster)
- Synagogue; Mosque (Synagoge; Moschee)
- Palace, Castle; Ruin (Schloss, Burg; Ruine)
- Tower; Lighthouse (Turm; Leuchtturm)
- Watermill; Windmill (Wassermühle; Windmühle)
- Power station (Kraftwerk)
- Mine; Cave (Bergwerk; Höhle)
- Monument (Denkmal)
- Airport (Flughafen)
- Other sight of interest (sonstige Sehenswürdigkeit)
- Museum (Museum)
- Excavations; Roman site (Ausgrabungen; röm. Objekte)
- Zoo; Nature info (Tierpark; Naturpark-Information)
- Nature reserve/Monument (Naturpark, -denkmal)
- Natural sight of interest (sonstige Natursehenswürdigkeit)
- Panoramic view* (Aussichtspunkt*)
- Tourist information; Restaurant (Tourist-Info; Gasthaus)
- Hotel, Guesthouse; Youth hostel (Hotel, Pension; Jugendherberge)
- Campground; Simple tent site* (Camping-; Lagerplatz*)
- Shopping facility*; Kiosk* (Einkaufsmöglichkeit*; Kiosk*)
- Picnic tables*; Covered stand* (Rastplatz*; Unterstand*)
- Outdoor pool; Indoor pool (Freibad; Hallenbad)
- Drinking fountain*; Parking lot* (Brunnen*; Parkplatz*)
- Schönern Picturesque town (sehenswertes Ortsbild)
- Facilities available (Einrichtung im Ort vorhanden)

Topographic information (Topographische Informationen)

- Church; Chapel (Kirche; Kapelle)
- Monastery/Convent (Kloster)
- Synagogue; Mosque (Synagoge; Moschee)
- Palace, Castle; Ruin (Schloss, Burg; Ruine)
- Tower; Lighthouse (Turm; Leuchtturm)
- Watermill; Windmill (Wassermühle; Windmühle)
- Power station, Solar power station (Kraftwerk)
- Mine; Cave (Bergwerk; Höhle)
- Monument; Burial mound (Denkmal; Hügelgrab)
- Airport; Airfield (Flughafen; Flugplatz)
- Windturbine (Windkraftanlage)
- TV/Radio tower (Funk- und Fernsehanlage)
- Transformer station (Umspannwerk, Trafostation)
- Wayside cross; Boundary stone (Wegkreuz; Grenzstein)
- Playing field, Stadium (Sportplatz, Stadion)
- Golf course; Tennis courts (Golfplatz; Tennisplatz)
- Boat landing; Sluice/lock (Schiffsanleger; Schleuse)
- Natural spring (Quelle)
- Wastewater treatment plant (Kläranlage)
- International border crossing (Staatsgrenze; Übergang)
- State border (Landesgrenze)
- District border (Kreis-, Bezirksgrenze)
- Nature reserve, National park (Naturschutzgebiet, Naturpark, Nationalpark)
- Prohibited zone (Truppenübungsplatz, Sperrgebiet)

- Motorway/Freeway; Expressway (Autobahn; Schnellstr.)
- Highway (Fernverkehrsstraße)
- Main road (Hauptstraße)
- Secondary main road (untergeordnete Hauptstraße)
- Secondary road; Access road (Nebenstraße; Fahrweg)
- Track; Ferry (Weg; Fähre)
- Road planned/under construction (geplant/in Bau)
- Railway/station; S-train station (Eisenbahn/Bahnhof; S-Bahnhof)
- Railway disused; planned (Eisenbahn stillgelegt; geplant)
- Narrow gauge railway (Schmalspurbahn)
- Mountain railway; Cable car (Bergbahn; Seilbahn)
- Forest; Park (Wald, Parkanlage)
- Marsh/Bog; Heath (Sumpf; Heide)
- Vineyards; Allotment gardens* (Weinbau; Gärten*)
- Cemetery; Dunes/Beach (Friedhof; Düne, Strand)
- Tidal flats; Glacier (Watt; Gletscher)
- Rock; Cliff; Scree (Felsen; Geröll)
- Quarry; Open cast mine* (Steinbruch, Tagebau*)
- Commercial/Industrial area (Gewerbe-, Industriegebiet)
- Urban area; Public building (Siedlung; öffentl. Gebäude)
- Defensive wall/Wall (Stadtmauer, Mauer)
- Embankment, Dike (Damm, Deich)
- Canal (Kanal)
- River/Dam/Lake (Fluss/Staumauer/See)
- Contour line 100m/50m (Höhenlinie 100m/50m)
- UTM-grid (2 km-grid) (UTM-Gitter)

5

Inhalt

City maps

The German Danube

Donau-Radwanderweg

Donauradweg

The Danube is not merely one of Europe's great rivers. At 2,888 kilometers from the source of the Breg and 2,845 kilometers from the confluence of the Breg, Brigach and Danube Spring in Donaueschingen, it is the second longest river in Europe; only the Volga (3,534 kilometers) is longer. It is one thousand kilometers longer than the Rhine, and collects water from a catchment basin that is more than four times as large. The Danube flows through or along the borders of ten nations and has long served as one of the most important transportation links between Europe and Asia.

Let us follow the Danube from its modest beginnings in southwestern Germany. Deep in the Black Forest, a few kilometers northwest of Furtwangen, the map notes the source of the Danube. If one follows this tiny stream, it reaches the village of Zindelstein, where it acquires a name: the Breg. It keeps this name as far as Donaueschingen, where it meets a second stream, the Brigach, coming from near Triberg to the north. The two streams merge and acquire a new name, the Danube (Donau in German), which it keeps in various forms and languages all the way to the Black Sea. The Danube is unique in Europe for another reason. As the only river in the continent which measures its kilometers from the mouth towards the source, it "ends" in Donaueschingen. In the 19th century, the residents of Donaueschingen erected an impressive basin around a karst-spring in the city's Schlosspark and declared it the river's source. This basin is decorated with a marble sculpture that shows the Danube as a small girl next to a woman who represents the Baar, the rolling hill coun-

try that surrounds the city. The Baar points the girl eastward towards the sea. The site does little to suggest a great river, however, as the waters from this purported "source" immediately disappear between metal bars into underwater pipes leading to the nearby Brigach.

Downstream from Donaueschingen, the Danube has barely begun its meandering march eastward when it reaches the foothills of the Swabian Alb near the town of Immendingen. This plateau is formed of porous limestone and provides the conditions for a remarkable and curious phenomenon called the Danube Sink. With a spooky gurgling and hissing, the river's waters disappear into the ground and flow beneath the surface until they reemerge 12 kilometers further East.

The banks of the Danube offer a rich diversity of natural and cultural sights. In Mühlheim, for instance, the medieval Enzberger castle and curious St. Gallus church look down on the river. Rocky promontories rise above the valley floor and provide habitat for many unusual birds and plants.

Ancient strongholds and castles keep guard over the river from strategic points along the valley. There is the massive Beuron Archabbey, for instance, built by the Austrian architect Franz Beer, or nearby Wildenstein

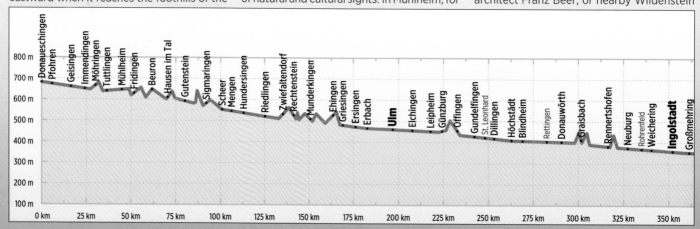

Castle where the hard-drinking Count Gott-fried von Zimmer sought refuge from the Black Plague in 1528 and thus also avoided the peasant uprisings that followed. Weren-wag Castle is where the minstrel Hugo von Werenwag wrote his verse around 1260. Nearby Kreenheinstetten was the birthplace in 1644 of Johann Ulrich Megerle, who later became famous in Vienna as the eloquent preacher Abraham a Sancta Clara. Each of these castles offers interesting views of the valley that the Danube has carved into the jurassic rock.

The valley widens near Inzigkofen before the river reaches Sigmaringen, where a proud castle, the one-time residence of the Hohen-zollerns, rises above a confusion of ancient roofs. From Sigmaringen the river continues in leisurely loops before emerging from the Swabian Alb at Ulm.

On its way to the Ingolstadt basin your cycling tour passes through a number of particularly scenic areas, including the Leibi nature pre-serve near Günzburg, many pristine flood plain areas, past Donauried and Donaumoos. This stretch of the ride also visits the charming towns of Dillingen, Gundelfingen, the renais-sance city of Neuburg, and Vohburg with its city walls and gates, before entering the Danube Gorge between Weltenburg and Kelheim.

From Regensburg, the Danube is navigable by ships and meets the Rhein-Main-Danube canal, which emerges from the Altmühl valley. With its 18 locks, the canal passes through the Upper Palatinate and Franconia to enable river traffic to travel from the North Sea to the Black Sea. The character of the Danube's valley also changes at Regensburg, which is the northern-most city along the river. North of the river, the Bavarian Forest rises away toward the Czech border and the central German highlands. To the South, the fertile soils of Bavaria's breadbasket extend towards the foothills of the Alps.

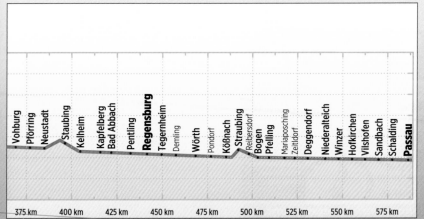

The Danube leaves Germany at Passau, the three-rivers city situated at the confluence of the Danube, Inn and Ilz rivers. They join to make the Danube qualify as a great river worthy of legend and fame.

The route

Length

The Danube cycling route between Donaueschingen and Passau is about 580 kilometers in length, not including about 210 kilometers of alternative routes and excursions.

Surface quality and traffic

Most of the route follows quiet country lanes or dedicated cycling paths. Sections with heavier traffic are rare and usually short. With only a few exceptions, the roads and paths have a hard surface. Gravel sections are usually in good condition. Because the route follows the course of the river, it is almost completely flat. It is mostly on the excursions into the surrounding countryside that must expect some steep sections. It is possible that during flooding part of the route is unusable or closed and you need to use alternative routes.

Signage

Signposting along the Danube bicycle route is generally reliable and signs are located at every change in direction at forks and intersections.

From Donaueschingen to Neustadt the signs are yellow with green lettering. Downstream from Neustadt the signs are white with green lettering. After Kelheim the signs also bear the slogan "Tour de Baroque" and the German Danube icon alternates with the lute-player seen on the Tour de Baroque signs.

Planing your tour

Central information sources

Arbeitsgemeinschaft Deutsche Donau, 86633 Neuburg a. d. Donau, Ottheinrichplatz A118, ☎ 08431/908330, www.deutsche-donau.de

Oberschwaben Tourismus GmbH., D-88427 Bad Schussenried, Neues Kloster 1, ☎ 07583/331060, www.oberschwaben-tourismus.de

Arrival & departure by air

Visitors from countries beyond Europe can reach Germany easily with commercial airlines. Once you have arrived in Europe, trains and buses offer excellent alternatives to air travel.

Arrival & departure by rail

The starting point of the Danube Bike Trail, Donaueschingen, can be easily reached by rail; from Munich about 4 hrs, from Stuttgart about 2 hrs and from Frankfurt 3 to 4 hrs.

For the return trip from Passau you have good rail connections; to München about 2 hrs, to Stuttgart 4 to 5 hrs.

Advance reservations are recommended, and are required at least one day in advance on most long-distance trains that accept bicycles in Germany. Due to the constantly changing prices and conditions for transport of a bicycle by rail we suggest that you inform yourself about your personal rail travel at the following addresses.

German Rail (DB):

General Service Number: ☎ 0180/6996633
Timetable Information: ☎ 0800/1507090
(€ 0.20/call from landline, mobile max. € 0.60/call)

www.bahn.de, www.bahn.de/bahnundbike

Bicycle transport

Hermes-Privat-Service:

☎ 0900/1311211 (€ 0,60/Min.)
www.myhermes.de; For information and oline booking go to the link Gepäck & Fahrrad.

Bike & train

Almost all the towns along the Danube valley are served by rail. If necessary or desired, you can easily take a train for sections of the route. The German states of Baden Württemberg and Bavaria offer "state tickets" for inexpensive train travel on regional trains.

Bicycle rentals:

Bicycles can be rented at the following train stations along the route:

Donaueschingen

Rad Center Rothweiler, Max-Egonstr. 11 (500m north of railway station), 78166 Donaueschingen, 0771/13148. Bicycle return anywhere along the route to passau.

Regensburg

Bikeambulanz - Bikehaus Regensburg, Regensburg railway station, west building, Bahnhofstraße 18, 93047 Regensburg, ☎ 0049 (0)941 599 88 08

Passau

Bikeambulanz - Bikehaus Passau, Passau railway station, west wing, Bahnhofstraße 29, 94032 Passau, ☎ 0049 (0)851 966 25 70

You should always inquire in advance about prices and opening hours at bicycle rentals. Rental fees vary from € 9 to € 14 per day.

Bike & ship

Excursion steamers on the Danube offer another interesting alternative to riding the entire stretch by bicycle. Ships stop in Kelheim, Regensburg and Passau. Addresses and schedules are reviewed in the town descriptions that follow in this guide.

There is also scheduled passenger service by ship between Deggendorf and Passau. Ship operators and addresses can be found in the town descriptions. Danube passenger ships do carry bicycles. For current departure and arrival times inquire at the ship landings or call the ship operators (for instance Wurm+Köck, D-94032 Passau, Höllg. 26, ☎ 0851/929292,

Fax: 35518, E-Mail: info@donauschiffahrt.de, www.donauschiffahrt.de).

The 5-kilometer section of the Danube bicycle route between Weltenburg and Kelheim is not to be recommended. It follows busy roads and has a long climb. The ships and boats that shuttle between Weltenburg and Kelheim offer an attractive alternative, and also enable you to enjoy the spectacular narrow gorge from the river. The ships run frequently during the summer season (daily every half-hour between 10 am and 6 pm, information ☏ 09441/5858, Kelheim office).

Overnight accommodation

A comprehensive list of overnight accommodation is provided at the end of this book. We have endeavoured to put together the largest possible choice of providers for you. The following internet addresses of accommodation providers, who also provide alternative types of accommodation, are recommended for those who are looking for alternatives or even more choice:

ADFC-Dachgeber works on the principle of reciprocal benefit: Here you find offers of private accommodation for cycling enthusiasts by cycling enthusiasts. More under www.dachgeber.de.

The **Deutsche Jugendherbergswerk** introduces itself and its 14 national associations under www.djh.de.

Also the **Naturfreunde** offer an alternative form of accommodation with their Naturfreunde Houses. More under www.naturfreunde.de. You will find just the **camping ground** you are looking for under www.camping-in.de or www.campingplatz.de.

Additionally, you will find further information about the ADFC listed **Bett+Bike** providers all over Germany under www.bettundbike.de.

Bicycle tours with children

Generally children over the age of 10 will be able to ride most of the routes detailed in the guide. Do not overestimate a child's stamina, however, and keep open options like taking a train or ship for some section of the trip.

Depending on their physical condition, most children can easily manage distances of 30 to 50 kilometers in a day. But remember that most children will not ride safely and with full concentration for hours on end. Finally, no child will enjoy the ride if his or her bicycle is poorly adjusted, heavy or poorly equipped for long distances. If riding with children in a trailer you will find the route near the start between Fridingen and Sigmaringen or between Rennertshofen and Neuburg somewhat difficult.

Bicycle to-ur operators

EUROBIKE Touristik GmbH, Mühlstr. 20, A-5162 Obertrum am See, ☏ 0043/6219/7444, Fax: 0043/6219/8272, www.eurobike.at, eurobike@eurobike.at
Austria Radreisen GmbH & CoKG, Joseph-Haydn-Str. 8, A-4780 Schärding, ☏ 0043/7712/55110, Fax: 0043/7712/4811, www.austria-radreisen.at, office@austria-radreisen.at
SwissTrails GmbH, Trockenloostrasse 101, 8105 Regensdorf, ☏ 0041 (0)43 4226022,

Fax: 0041 (0)43 4226011,
info@swisstrails.ch, www.swisstrails.ch
Flusskulturreisen, Waldweg 54,
D-06846 Dessau-Roßlau, ✆ 0340/2214881,
www.flusskulturreisen.de
PEDALO Touristik GmbH, Kickendorf 1a,
A-4710 Grieskirchen, ✆ 0043/7248/635840,
Fax: 0043/7248/635844, www.pedalo.com,
info@pedalo.com
Augustus Tours, Turnerweg 6,
D-01097 Dresden, ✆ 0049/351/563480,
Fax: 0049/351/5634800,
www.augustustours.de,
info@augustustours.de
Rückenwind Reisen GmbH,
Am Patentbusch 14, D-26125 Oldenburg,
✆ 0441/48597-0, Fax: 0441/48597-23,
www.rueckenwind.de,
info@rueckenwind.de

About this Book

This cycling guide contains all the information you need for your cycling vacation along the Danube Bike Trail between Donaueschingen and Passau: Precise maps, a detailed description of the route in both directions, a comprehensive list of overnight accommodation, numerous detail maps of cities and towns, and information about the most significant sights. And all that information comes with our bikeline pledge: The route described in this book has been tested and evaluated in person by one of our editors! To assure that the book is as up-to-date as possible, we welcome corrections submitted by readers and local officials or businesses. We cannot, however, always check and confirm such changes before deadline.

The tour is not divided into day stages, but into logical sections, as the daily accomplishment depends too much upon how fit each rider is or how casually you wish to tackle the tour.

The maps

A map at the inside of the front page provides you with an overview of the geographical area in which the tour in this book is situated. The outlines and numbers of the individual detail maps are also given.

The detail maps are produced at a scale of 1:50,000 (1 centimeter = 500 meters). In addition to exactly describing the route, these maps also provide information about roadway quality (paved or unpaved), climbs (gentle or steep), distances, as well as cultural and natural attractions and facilities along the route. Be aware that there may be some difference between actual and given distances due to rounding.

With even the most precise maps it may be necessary to consult the written description of the route at times. Locations where the route is difficult to follow are shown by the ⚠ symbol on the maps, the same symbol can then be found in the written description where the route is explained in detail.

Note that the recommended main route is always shown in red or purple; alternative and excursion routes in orange. The individual symbols used in the maps are described in the legend on pages 4 and 5.

Route altitude profile

The altitude profile given in the introduction provides you with an overview of the elevations, the length and the location of towns and cities along the route.

Additionally, a more detailed altitude profile is given at the beginning of each section. This profile also includes waypoints, providing a direct correlation to the detail maps and route descriptions. which gives you , including provides a graphic depiction of elevations along the route, the total length, and the location of larger It does not show every individual small hill and dip, but only the major changes in elevation. On the detail maps smaller gradients are shown by arrows that point uphill.

The text

The maps are supplemented by a written text that describes the route starting in Prague and proceeding down the Vltava and Elbe rivers

to Magdeburg. Key phrases about the route description are indicated with the ～ symbol. Many distinctive or important positions along the route are marked as waypoints with consecutive numbers **1**, **2**, **3**, ... and, to help with navigation, are to be found with the same symbol in the maps.

The description of the main route is also interrupted by passages describing alternative and excursion routes. These are printed in orange colour.

Furthermore, the names of important villages, towns and cities are printed in bold type. If a location or community has important points of interest, addresses, telephone numbers and opening times are listed in the blue text blocks.

Descriptions of the larger towns and cities, as well as historic, cultural and natural landmarks help round out the travel experience. These paragraphs are printed in italics to distinguish them from the route description.

ALTERNATIVE Text printed in purple indicates that you must make a decision about how your tour shall continue. For instance, there may be an

alternative route that is not included in the tour description, or a turn-off to another location. **EXCURSION** These also indicate excursion suggestions, interesting sights or recreational facilities that are not directly on the main route.

List of overnight accommodation

The last pages of this cycling guide provide a list of convenient hotels and guest houses in virtually every village or town along the route. This list also includes youth hostels and camping grounds.

Donaueschingen to Ulm

The first section of this ride passes through especially scenic landscapes. The Danube, which is little more than a stream at this point, curves in leisurely loops across the countryside. Near Geisingen the valley narrows, and the river's meandering course becomes ever more impressive. Tall limestone cliffs with romantic pinnacles line the valley. An unusual spectacle is the Danube Sink between in the Upper Danube Nature preserve between Immendingen and Möhringen. The river then winds along the southern edge of the Swabian Alb, passing numerous castles, abbeys and palaces. Especially impressive: the castle Wildenstein, Beuron Archabbey and the Hohenzollern castle at Sigmaringen.

The route follows mostly flat terrain and is generally well-paved. The only climbs and gravel stretches come in the narrow Danube valley. Downstream from Sigmaringen, the river becomes wider as it passes through a broad valley. In Ehingen you can turn your back on the Danube and follow an alternative route through the Blau valley. Ulm with its old city and huge cathedral offers a fitting end to this stage.

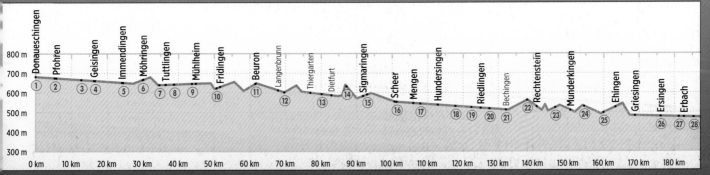

The Danube Source

"Brigach and Breg set the Danube on its way" goes an old classroom rhyme to help geography students with their lessons. But it does not completely explain the source of Europe's second-longest river. The Breg carries more water and is longer than the Brigach, and it was at the Breg's source near Furtwangen that locals placed a small monument marking the spot as the Danube's source. When residents of Furtwangen applied to have "their" Danube source

officially recognized in 1965, city leaders in Donaueschingen were not amused. After all, the Roman emperor Tiberius had long ago recognized a spring in the city's Fürstenberg Park as the Danube's source. The dispute was settled in that the official Danube spring was allowed to remain in Donaueschingen, while the Breg spring was marked on maps as the Danube's headwaters.

Donaueschingen

Postal Code: 78166; Area code: 0771

- 🛈 **Tourist Information**, Karlstr. 58, ✆ 857-221, www.donaueschingen.de
- 🏛 **Fürstenberg Collections**, Karlspl. 7, ✆ 229677563, Open: Apr.-Nov., Tue-Sat 10-13 & 14-17, Sun/Hol 10-17.
- 🏛 **Museum Biedermann**, Museumsweg 1, ✆ 896689-0, Open: Tue-Sun 11-17.
- 🏛 **Kinder- und Jugendmuseum (Children's Museum)**, Haldenstr. 5, ✆ 92947426, Open: Tue-Fri 14-17:30, Sat, Sun/Hol 10-17:30
- ⛪ **Fürstlich Fürstenbergisches Schloss**, ✆ 229677560, Guided tours, Info by 🛈, groups by arrangement.

- ⛪ **St. Johann**, Bohemian baroque church.
- ✉ **Park public pool**, ✆ 4186, Open: Late May-early Sept., Mon-Sun 9-20.
- 🚲 **Rad Center Rothweiler**, Max-Egonstr. 11, ✆ 13148

The name Fürstenberg has long been associated with the city of Donaueschingen. The German baronial family has left numerous marks

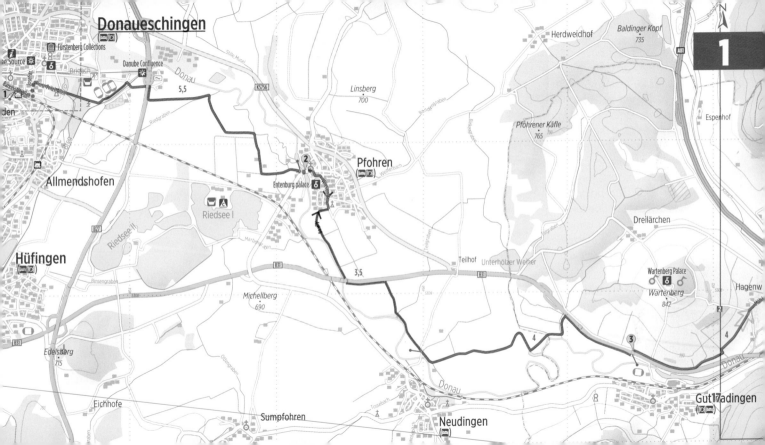

on the city, which has been the family's residence since 1723. There is the Fürstenberg Brewery and the Fürstlich Fürstenberg Palace near St. Johann, a Bohemian baroque church. The palace park is also the location of the Danube spring, an artfully constructed basin decorated with figures representing the Mother Baar who points the young maiden Danube toward the east. The spring can also be reached from Josefstraße and Straße An der Stadtkirche.

Donaueschingen Town hall and fountain

Donaueschingen to Geisingen — 17 km

1 The tour begins from the train station in Donaueschingen ~ turn right on **Bahnhofstraße** and proceed to the roundabout ~ take the second exit, **Josefstraße** (here are signs for the Donauquelle) ~ at the next T-intersection turn right into **Prinz Fritzi Allee** ~ and ride through the palace park ~ keep right after the transformer station.

TIP From here you will be guided by the small yellow signs marked "Donau-Radwanderweg" and the "Deutsche Donau" logo.
Proceed for a short time along Breg Creek until you reach the bridge.

TIP To reach the confluence of the Brigach and Breg, follow the path along the creek which begins just after the bridge.
Turn right over the bridge across the Breg ~. continue under the **B 27** ~ immediately turn right before the wastewater treatment plant ~ follow the paved path between fields to Pfohren ~ **2** at the intersection turn left onto the **K 5749**, which takes you across the Danube and into the village of Pfohren.

Pfohren

6 **Entenburg palace**, the former waterpalace was built in 1471 by Count Heinrich von Fürstenberg as a hunting palace.

In the village turn right on **Entenburgweg** ~ ride past the **Entenburg** hunting palace ~ turn right on **Wiesenstraße** ~ at the edge of the village turn right into the paved field road ~ this takes you under the main road ~ follow the paved field road, at first beside the main road, then right ~ continue straight at the 5-way intersection by the river, not crossing the bridge ~ keep left by the building and continue to the main road ~ **3** follow the route along the B 31and through the underpass towards Geisingen.

Brigach and Breg confluence

The young Danube

Wartenberg

On the left you can see the 821 meter Wartenberg. It is one of the extinct Hegau volcanos and offers fine views into the surrounding landscape. The lords of Wartenberg and of Fürstenberg, whose castles stood on opposite sides of the Danube, fought each other for centuries until Count Heinrich II of Fürstenberg got tired of the feud and married the last female member of the Wartenberg line around 1300. It was a shrewd move, which ended the rivalry and enabled the Fürstenbergs to take over all Wartenberg possessions.

Continue straight along the paved field road ～ as you reach Geisingen turn right at the T-intersection ～ immediately right again onto the **Hauptstraße**.

Geisingen

Postal Code: 78187; Area code: 07704

- ℹ **Rathaus**, Hauptstr. 36, ☏ 8070
- **Wartenberg.** The hill of the same name carries the ruins of two early castles and a palace from 1780.
- **Kreuzkirche Pilgrimage Church** (18th c.), houses the lifesize figure of Jesus on the cross, which still carries a lead shot said to have been shot into his forehead during the thirty years war.
- **Arena-Geisingen**, Am Espen 16, ☏ 922287. Germany's first covered inlineskating arena lies in a park by the Danube.
- **Bühler Technik GmbH**, Kleine Breite 2, ☏ 92850

Geisingen is one of the oldest towns in the Baar plateau, being first mentioned in deeds from the monastery of St. Gallen in 724. According to documents, the town of Geisingen was founded beside the village of the same name around 1300 by the Counts von Wartenberg. The first mention of the town dates to 1329, as the Wartenberger property went to the Counts von Fürstenberg after the Wartenberger line died out in 1321.

Geisingen to Tuttlingen — 18.8 km

Ride through the centre of Geisingen ～ turn right at the second roundabout ～ **4** cross the railway tracks ～ immediately left onto the bicycle path ～ follow the path beside the tracks ～ you pass underneath the freeway and the **B 31** ～ under a railway bridge ～ by the house turn right across the Danube ～ left onto the bicycle path at the T-intersection ～ turn right into Hintschingen.

Hintschingen

Follow the **Ortsstraße** through the village, turning left before it becomes the **Schöntalstraße** ～ follow the field road to a covered wooden bridge ～ cross the bridge ～ keep right at the forks to stay on the paved lane beside railway line ～ continue along the tracks to the Immendingen railway station.

Immendingen

Postal Code: 78194; Area code: 07462

- ℹ **Tourist-Information**, Schlosspl. 2, ☏ 24228
- **Heimatmuseum (Local museum)**, Hindenburgstr. 2, Open: by arrangement with the council office: ☏ 24-0

3

Unterer Berg
870

Wurmlingen

Papiermühle

Nendingen

Ludwigstal

Tuttlingen

Koppenland

Honberg Ruin

Ehrenberg
770

Gallertalhof

Möhringen Vorstadt

Maiental

Gänsäcker

Möhringen

Hostel

Danube Seepage by Immendingen

6 Upper palace, Schlosspl. 2, extended since its 12th c beginning, serving as a factory in the 19th c, now houses the town hall.

Take the pedestrian and bicycle bridge across the tracks ~ after the bridge turn right on the bike path that leads into **Blumenweg** ~ turn right on **Donaustraße** ~ continue straight and **5** cross the Danube on the bicycle bridge ~ continue straight on the side street ~ along the railroad tracks ~ after the wastewater treatment plant turn left across another bicycle bridge over the Danube ~ keep right onto the paved lane before the railway tracks.

The Danube Seepage

Just a few kilometers after the Danube starts to look like a real river, it seems to magically disappear into the ground with a mysterious gurgling and splashing. When the river is low, the riverbed above ground dries up completely as the river seeps into the porous limestone layers beneath the soil. For about 12 kilometers the Danube's waters wind through an underground labyrinth of caves and channels. It resurfaces at Germany's largest spring, the Aachtopf, where some 10,000 litres bubble up out of the ground every second to form the Aach, which flows down to Lake Constance and into the Rhine. The water spends an average of about 60 hours underground in the Danube Sink, though some of the water has been shown to take weeks and even months to resurface.

People used salt and dyes as early as 1877 to investigate the underground river. The first places where the river vanishes into the ground are visible as an earthen funnel on the south bank near the Immendingen railroad bridge. Whirlpools form there when the water is high. During the summer months, if the water is low, one can find fantastic stone formations on a walk along the dry river bed to Möhringen. Although the caves form one of Europe's largest underground river systems, divers and researchers have explored only a small part of the network.

To assure that some of the Danube's water reaches downstream communities, a canal was built between Immendingen and Möhringen to carry some of the Danube's water around the sink and into the Danube valley. Continue along the tracks to Möhringen.

Möhringen

Postal Code: 78532; Area code: 07462

ℹ Tourist-Info, Hermann-Leiber-Str. 4, ☎ 948220 (former hunting palace).

Möhringen

Tuttlingen

🏛 **Museum im Rathaus**, Hermann-Leiber-Str. 4, Open: Mon-Fri 8-11, Mon-Thur 14-16. Local history and musical instruments collection.

🏛 **Steam Locomotive Museum**, in the train house (towards Tuttlingen), Open: May-3rd Oct., Sun/Hol 10-17.

❌ **History trail**, from the town hall, ✆ 948210

The earliest documented reference to Möhringen dates from the year 882, and in 1308 it gained city and market status. In 1470, Austrian Emperor Friedrich II awarded the city its coat of arms showing a Moor. Its name comes from "Moringas," or city of Moring, a local ruler.

6 At the first intersection in Möhringen turn left across the tracks ~ and then immediately right on **Hermann Leiber Straße** ~ pass the tourist

information and the museum ~ keep right on **Marktgasse** ~ turn left on **Am Schafmarkt**. Proceed straight across the main road into **Gihrsteinstraße** ~ turn right on **Anton Braun Straße** and then left on **Bleichestraße** ~ at the T-intersection right on **Am Mühlberg** ~ continue into the gravel road along the edge of the woods ~ you come to follow the river into the suburb of Koppenland ~ continue into the paved bicycle path along the river ~ **7** you pass the public pool ~ keep right across the creek and continue under several bridges along the Danube into the new **Donaupark**, which offers an attractive spot for a pause in the centre of Tuttlingen ~ continue to the wooden bridge.

CENTRE To reach the city's interesting pedestrian area, cross the Danube on the wooden bridge **Rathaussteg**.

Tuttlingen

Postal Code: 78532; Area code: 07461

ℹ **Touristinfo Tuttlingen**, Rathausstr. 1, ✆ 99340, www.tuttlingen.de

🏛 **Museum Tuttlinger Haus**, Donaustr. 19, ✆ 15135, Open: Easter-1st Nov., Tue, Thur, Sat, Sun 14-17.

🏛 **Museum Fruchtkasten**, Donaustr. 50, ✆ 15135, Open: Open: Tue, Thur, Sat, Sun 14-17. Town and industry history, archaeology and more.

🏛 **Gallery**, Rathausstr. 7, ✆ 99318, Open: Tue-Sun/Hol. 11-18. Changing exhibitions of contemporary art.

⛪ **Lutheran city church**, Open: May-Sept. Sun-Thur 14-16.

❌ **Rathaus (Town Hall)**, From 1804, designed by Carl Leonhard von Uber.

📧 Tuttlingen **public pool**.

🛁 **TuWass**, Thermal and recreational baths, Mühlenweg 1-5, ✆ 9665566

📠 **Fa. Nerz**, Ludwigstaler Str. 77, ✆ 96000

☑ **Dangelmaier**, Oberamteistr. 26, ✆ 3019

☑ **Radler-Welt**, Goethestr. 1, ✆ 72001

After a catastrophic fire in 1803, Tuttlingen was rebuilt and emerged as an important district city with about 35,000 residents. The city's main attraction is the Lutheran church, which is one of the most beautiful art nouveau churches in Germany. Rising above the city is the Honberg, which is crowned by the ruins of an old castle and offers fine views onto the surrounding city.

Tuttlingen to Beuron   21.9 km

ALTERNATIVE If you do not wish to ride beside the road, you have the option of using a signposted bicycle path along the south bank of the river.

South bank alternative

Take the **Rathaussteg** across the Danube and then turn left on **Weimarstraße** and straight into the street **In Wöhrden**. Follow the south bank of the Danube to the first buildings in **Ludwigstal**, where you turn left across the river to the roundabout. Here you rejoin the main route on the bicycle path to the right.

To take the main route, pass the wooden bridge and continue beside the river 〜 you depart Tuttlingen on the bike path along the **Nendinger Allee** 〜 at the roundabout proceed straight and under the main road 〜 **8** turn right immediately after crossing the railway line 〜 follow the paved lane beside the tracks to Nendingen.

Nendingen

Postal Code: 78532; Area code: 07461

🛈 Touristinfo Tuttlingen, ✆ 99340

🏛 Agricultural Museum, Industriestr. 4, ✆ 3647, Open: daily. Exhibits of agricultural machinery.

Follow the lane to the right across the railway line 〜 turn right on **Industriestraße** 〜 at the next T-intersection turn left onto **Sattlerstraße** 〜 straight 〜 continue straight into the **Austraße**, a paved lane that takes you towards Stetten.

Stetten

⛪ St. Nikolaus parish church

ALTERNATIVE In Stetten you can either continue along the signposted main route or take a short excursion through the pretty medieval centre of Mühlheim.

Via Mühlheim

After crossing the Kesselbach turn right into **Rathausstraße** 〜 right on **Donaustraße** 〜 cross the Danube 〜 along the bicycle path under the **L 443** 〜 keep left onto **Tuttlinger Straße** 〜 turn left into the right bend to reach the historic centre.

Mühlheim an der Donau

Postal Code: 78570; Area code: 07463

🛈 **Verkehrsamt**, Vorderes Schloss, ✆ 8903, www.muehlheim-donau.de

🏛 **Museum**, Vorderes Schloss, Open: Sun 14-17. Local history.

⛪ **Gallus church**, the oldest church in Mühlheim (10th-11th c.), its 14th-15th c. frescos and the adjacent **Veitskapelle** are worth seeing.

⛪ **Maria Hilf Church Ruin**, on the Welschenberg

✹ **Town Hall**, Hauptstr. 16, is one of the oldest buildings in the town. Parts of it are believed to date back to 1200.

✹ **Mühlheim night watch**: From 1496-1936 a night watchman patrolled the city and announced the time every hour. In the 1990 Siegfried Kunz revived that tradition on weekends in the summer months.

The picturesque old city of Mühlheim is visible from afar perched on a ridge above the Danube.

Kolbingen

Reinfelderhof

Beuron

St. Maurus

Beuron Monastery

11

Hintelestal Nature Reserve

Gansnestweg

Kolbinger Cave

Hammerschmiede

Virgin Mary Grotto 1,6

Wacholderbühl
755

2,4

Schönenberg
835

Mühlheimer Cave

Gelber Fels

3,5

Galgenberg

Gallus Chapel

5,7

Gansniest Lookout

Schafberg
835

Schlasberg

Mühlheim
a.d. Donau

Hennbühl
695

Bronnen Palace

Bronnen

Schnellenberg
860

Donau

Stetten

10

Fridingen
a.d. Donau

0,8

9

Maria Hilf-Church Ruin

Welschenberg
815

Kirchberg
795

Scharf Eck
Local Museum

Ifflinger Palace

Skihütte

4

Ettenberg
750

Stiegelesfels

3,8

2,5

Laibfelsen

Schänzle
680

Buchhe

Bergsteig

Ziegelhütte

Kallenberg

25

Donau

Nendingen

Scheilenbühl
810

Mühlheim an der Donau, Torplatz

If you have a weakness for romantic old cities, you should find the strength to pedal up the steep but short road to the upper city. The narrow streets and half-timbered houses with pointed roofs are built on a rocky ledge and surrounded by the old city wall. During much of the year, colourful flowers line the window sills to complete the quaint atmosphere.

The first known mention of Mühlheim can be found in a document dated 799 from the Reichenau abbey. Mühlheim was awarded city status in 1300, and in 1409 the brothers Friedrich and Engelhardt von Enzberg purchased

authority over the city from the Weitingen Knights. Descendents of the von Enzbergs still live here today.

Take the **Hauptstraße** through the historic centre of Mühlheim ⁓ follow the right bend and descend to the valley floor along the street **An der Steig** ⁓ at the roundabout take the exit L 443(Bahnhofstraße).

Stetten

To stay on the main route through Stetten go straight on **Bachstraße** ⁓ **9** take **Josef Lang Straße** across the bridge over the tracks ⁓ turn right onto the bicycle path along **Eisenbahnstraße** ⁓ keep right to follow the path along the railway line into Mühlheim.

Mühlheim a. d. Donau   see previous page

Straight on **Griesweg** ⁓ at the T-intersection, where the excursion rejoins the main route from the right, turn left onto **Kolbinger Straße(L 443)** ⁓ at the edge of town turn right into a paved lane ⁓ follow the lane between scattered houses ⁓ turn right just after the Gallus church and cemetery ⁓ the narrow, paved lane takes you through a beautiful nature reserve ⁓ continue

between fields and forest and then along the Danube to Fridingen ⁓ continue beside the river to the main road ⁓ **10** turn right onto a bicycle path along the road ⁓ after 300 m turn right into the street **Oberer Damm**.

ALTERNATIVE To ride through the historic centre of Fridingen you can leave the main route briefly and take the follow route.

Continue straight along the Bahnhofstraße ⁓ turn left after the Gasthof Sonne ⁓ keep left into Mittlere Gasse ⁓ left into Gartenstraße ⁓ turn right at Friedenstraße ⁓ turn left onto Unteren Damm to rejoin the main route.

Fridingen
Postal Code: 78567; Area code: 07463

- 🛈 **Donau-Heuberg**, Verkehrsamt im Rathaus, Kirchplatz 2, ☎ 8370, www.donau-heuberg.de
- 🏛 **Local museum Oberes Donautal**, in the Ifflinger Schloss, ☎ 8474, Open: Sun/Hol 14-18.
- 🏛 **Artists House "Scharf Eck"**, Kirchpl. 2, ☎ 99120555, Open: May-Oct., Sat, Sun/Hol 14-18. Three generations of the artist family Bucher lived here in the oldest and most beautiful town house in the Fridingen. On display are works of painters from the upper Danube valley.

"Scharf Eck" in Fridingen

❄ **Kolbinger Cave**, ☎ 97083, Open: Good Friday-Oct., Sat 13-17 and Sun 10-17.

♨ 🏊 **Hamma**, Tuttlinger Str. 14, ☎ 7703

The prettiest half-timbered house in the town is called Scharf Eck at the upper gate where the city wall stood. It was recently converted into an artists' house in which exhibition spaces document the life and work of the well-known Fridingen artist Hans Bucher. The Ifflinger Schloss contains an interesting local history museum, the Museum Oberes Donautal. If you have time and interest in theatre, the natural amphitheatre at Steintäle presents high-quality performances from June to September.

The route segment from Fridingen to Beuron goes through some of the most beautiful landscape along the German Danube. Rocky formations crowd the valley so that only the railroad and a simple track have room on the valley floor. Shining white limestone cliffs rise almost vertically and suggest the eons that the Danube needed to wear a course through the 300 meters tall stone formation.

Continue straight across the L 277 into the street **Unterer Damm**, directly along the Danube.

Keep right to continue along the river as you leave Fridingen ～ follow the left curve in the paved lane by the wastewater treatment plant ～ at the T-intersection, turn right across the bridge over the Danube ～ keep left after the bridge and continue to the left ～ keep left as you pass the **Scheuerlehof** ～ after another 3 km you reach the "Jägerhaus" inn.

EXCURSION A hiking trail starts at the inn and goes past the cave Jägerhaushöhle to the old castle, Burg Bronnen. The castle is not open to the public.

The next 3 km follow an unpaved forest track ～ after a gate the track is paved, ahead you can see the Monastery of Beuron ～ the paved lane takes you up a steep hill to the main road ～ **11** cross the road and then immediately turn right.

CENTRE To reach the Benediktine Monastery of Beuron simply continue straight across the bridge.

EXCURSION Wildenstein Castle, which also contains a youth hostel, can be reached by bicycle from Beuron via the K 8278 and Leibertingen. The first 5 km are quite steep, but thereafter the ride up to the castle is no problem.

Beuron Monastery

27

Beuron

Postal Code: 88631; Area code: 07466

ℹ Tourist-Information, Kirchstr. 18, Hausen, ✆ 07579/92100, www.beuron.de

🏛 Upper Danube Nature Protection Centre (Naturschutzzentrum Obere Donau), in the former railway station, Wolterstr. 16, ✆ 92800. Open: all year Mon-Fri, 9-17, and 1st Apr.-31st Oct., Sat, Sun/Hol., 13-17. Permanent exhibitions covering earth history, cultural history and natural landscapes in the Upper Danube Nature Reserve, as well as changing exhibitions.

🕀 Monastery Church. Open: daily, 5-20. Guided tours by arrangement ✆ 17175.

🕀 Benediktine Monastery St. Martin, ✆ 170. Active monastery which offers an insight into monastery life, courses and accommodation. Also houses a Bible Museum and Natural History Collection.

✹ Naturparkexpress, May-Oct., Sat, Sun/ Hol, ✆ 92800

The archabbey Beuron was mentioned as part of the possessions of the St. Gallen abbey as early as 861. The Benedictine monastery that stands there today was established in the 11th century as an Augustine abbey. The abbey has a long tradition of artistic and scientific study, and today generates its own electricity.

Beuron to Sigmaringen   30.7 km

The route between Beuron and Wildenstein runs along the Petersfelsen cliffs, with the Danube winding its way through the valley below ∼ after passing under the railway you cross the Danube ∼ after a short climb turn right ∼ continue past the St. Maurus chapel ∼ after the bridge turn left towards Sigmaringen.

EXCURSION If you wish to visit Wildenstein Castle, turn right here. The trail is a hiking path and takes about 30 minutes by foot to reach the castle.

Werenwag Palace

The upper reaches of the Danube, with its many valleys, hillsides and rocky outcrops, was well suited for medieval fortifications. Nowhere else does the Danube feature as many castles as on the short stretch between Donaueschingen and Sigmaringen. Possibly the most impressive of these bastions is Wildenstein Castle, perched high on a rocky summit. Known to have existed as early as 1077, the castle enjoyed its heyday in the 15 th and 16 th centuries. Today it ranks as the jewel of the Swabian Danube, having survived the turmoils of Europe's darkest periods thanks to its massive walls and double moat. It was only due to the occupants' carelessness that the Swedish armies were able to temporarily seize the castle in 1642.

This stretch of the cycle route passes many famous outcroppings, like the Bishop's rock, the Glasträger rock and the Kornelius rock near Hausen.

Follow the right bank of the Danube until you reach a parking area by the main road before

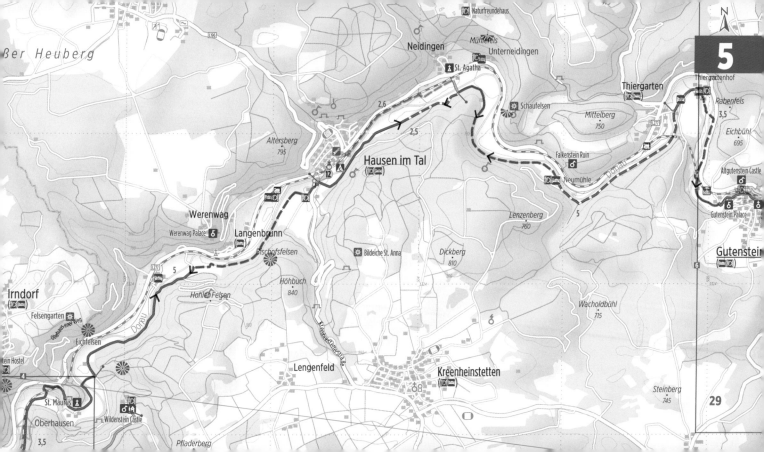

Ber Heuberg

Naturfreundehaus

Neidingen

Mühlfels

Unterneidingen

St. Agatha

2,6

Schaufelsen

Thiergarten

Thiergartenhof

Rabenfels
3,5

Altersberg
795

2,5

Mittelberg
750

Eichbühl
695

Hausen im Tal

Falkenstein Ruin

Altgutenstein Castle

12

Neumühle

Werenwag

5

Gutenstein Palace

Werenwag Palace

Langenbrunn

Bischofsfelsen

Lenzenberg
760

Gutenstei

Bildeiche St. Anna

Höhbuch
840

Dickberg
810

Hohlen Felsen

Donau

Irndorf

5

Wacholdbühl
715

Felsengarten

Obmaus ener Weg

Eichfelsen

6

Lengenfeld

Kreenheinstetten

Steinberg
745

tein Hostel

4

St. Maurus

Oberhausen

Wildenstein Castle

Pfladerberg

3,5

Hausen ~ keep left on the main road ~ **12** turn right just before you reach the bridge over the Danube.

ALTERNATIVE For those wishing to ride through Hausen im Tal, simply follow the alternative route given in the map. You will rejoin the main route across the bridge down from the railway crossing by Neidingen.

Hausen im Tal

Postal Code: 88631; Area code: 07579

i Tourist information, Kirchstr. 18, ✆ 92100

Eppinger, Hintere Dorfstr. 6, ✆ 933706

Continue along the right bank of the Danube ~ it is paved initially, then unpaved ~ and passes Neidingen on the opposite bank.

Neidingen

The poet Anton Schlude wrote the following about Neidingen in 1858:

"After the traveler has patiently poked around in the ruins of the old palace at Hausen and made his way back down the mountain, the tree-lined road along the left bank of the Danube leads him into the little hamlet of Neidingen not half-an-hour away ... Neidingen consists of

Inner Courtyard former Inzigkofen Abbey

three parts. Upper and Lower Neidingen and the five hillside houses across from the mountain on the road to Stetten. The 130 inhabitants, like those in Hausen, live exclusively from farming... . Further downstream from Neidingen there once stood Schaufels palace. The crag there still bears that name. But the most remarkable thing about Neidingen is that a city of the same name supposedly once occupied the right bank of the Danube, on a moderate hill named Buchtbühl, where ruins of old walls can still be found in the ground. What makes this legend yet more probable is that a 12 th century map documents

this Neidingen as a significant locale ... Another piece of evidence is that when the French first came to us in 1796, their maps also showed this Neidingen. Despite all that, however, we can do no more than voice our conjectures because there is no official document that names the place."
By the village of **Thiergarten** the Danube makes a large curve before it enters a narrow valley ~ at the end of this curve you cross the river ~ and follow the bicycle path into the village of Gutenstein.

Gutenstein

13 Turn left after the village church ~ cross the tracks and turn right on the unpaved track along the railway line ~ cross the bridge ~ and ride past Dietfurth with its ruins ~ through the gorge at Teufelsloch to the train station at Inzigkofen ~ turn right across the bridge ~ you must ride uphill on a busy road to Inzigkofen ~ the view from the top is excellent.

Inzigkofen

Postal Code: 72514; Area code: 07571

i Mayor's office Inzigkofen, Ziegelweg 2 ✆ 73070, www.inzigkofen.de

- 🏛 **Abbey Museum**, in the former Inzigkofen abbey, ✆ 73980
- 🏛 **Agricultural Museum (Bauernmuseum)**, ✆ 52415 (Mr. E. Beck)
- 🎱 **Inzigkofen Abbey**, the former Augustine abbey has served as an adult education centre since the middle of the 20th c.
- 🎱 **Former Abbey Church**.
- 🏞 **Educational herbal garden**, on the former abbey grounds, Open: May-Oct., Mon-Sun 9-19.
- 🏞 **Inzigkofer Park**, in the imposing gorge with its rough limestone cliffs. A network of footpaths and stairs lead to various sights. Of particular interest **Amalien rock**, the **Teufelsbrücke (devils bridge)**, **Känzele Lookout** and **caves**.

Inzigkofer Park

Bicycle tourists who have the time should not miss the opportunity to take a walk through the park in Inzighofen. It was built through the generosity of Count Anton von Hohenzollern, who wanted to give every citizen the possibility of exploring this spectacular terrain in a park-like setting. Riders can park their bicycles at the entrance and follow hiking paths towards the Amalien rock at the eastern end of the park. From the Amalien rock there is a steep path to the Teufelsbrücke (Devil's bridge). The bridge's name is said to have its origin in the following story. In 1843, when the Count Karl instructed his court architect to build a wooden bridge over the gorge, the architect told his master, "The devil can build it, but I won't!" No sooner had he spoken those words when the devil appeared and promised to build the bridge, but only under the condition that he be given the soul of the first to cross the finished structure. The deal was agreed, but when the bridge was completed, a dog was chased across the span and the devil was cheated of his prize. The concrete bridge that stands at the site today was built in 1895, apparently without satanic support.

Past the bridge, there is a small tunnel that leads to the Inzigkofen-Nickhof road. About 100 meters further a trail goes to the left over a meadow towards a woods and the "Känzele", a picturesque rocky point that offers fine views into the "Degerau" valley. From the Känzele the trail drops down to the "grottos," a mighty cave and rocky formations. Hikers can then proceed to a romantic stone gate up steps that lead to a wooded avenue back to the abbey.

14 In Inzigkofen turn left just past the abbey ~ follow the paved lane into the valley and over to Laiz.

Laiz

Continue along the Danube to Sigmaringen, where the mighty Hohenzollern palace looms above the small city's historic centre.

At the camping ground you have a choice of following the official route along the Danube or taking a detour through the city.

To ride through the city, turn right at the camping ground and proceed straight into the city. To continue along the main route, simply follow the path along the Danube.

Känzele lookout, Inzigkofen

Sigmaringen

Postal Code: 72488; Area code: 07571

ℹ **Tourist Info**, Leopoldpl. 4, ☏ 106224,
www.sigmaringen.de

🏛 **Fürstliches Museum**, Sigmaringen Palace, Karl-Anton-Pl. 8, ☏ 729230, Open: Nov.-Mar., 10-16, Apr.-Oct., 9-18. Exhibits from the private collections of the Princes of Hohenzollern include jewelery and accessories, musical instruments, arms and armour, paintings and documents, as well as a rich collection of Swabian paintings, sculptures and metalwork from the 15th and 16th centuries.

🏛 **Mattes-Zündapp-Museum**, Zoller-Hof Brewery, Leopoldstr. 40, ☏ 0173/61362277, Open: Apr.-Oct., Sat-Sun 13-17, Jul.-Sept., Thur-Sun 10-17. Over 100 exhibits of the legendary Nuremberg motorbike manufacturer Zündapp.

🏛 **Local History Museum "Runder Turm"** in a former defensive tower of the town fortifications, Open: Sat, Sun 14-17 and Jul.-Oct., also Wed 14-17. Entry is free.

🏰 **Schloss Sigmaringen**, Karl-Anton-Pl. 8, ☏ 729230, Open: Nov.-Mar., 10-16, Apr.-Oct., 9-18, guided tours only. A castle is first mentioned on the site in 1077, the oldest remains dating from around 1200, while the current complex dates mostly from renovations in the 17th and 19th c. It is the seat of the Princes of Hohenzollern-Sigmaringen, housing a museum as well as being open to guided tours.

🏊 **Sigmaringen outdoor pool**, heated public pool, ☏ 63474

✳ **Paddel & Pedale**, ☏ 2448, canoe trips through the Danube valley, with bicycle transfer.

The Sigmaringen royal Hohenzollern palace on a rocky outcrop above the Danube is built on the site of an 11th century castle that belonged to the Counts of Werdenberg. After a devastating fire in 1893, it was rebuilt in its current form by, among others, Emanuel von Seidl for the Hohenzollerns.

Sigmaringen to Mengen   15.7 km

15 From the Hedinger Church take **Badstraße** out of Sigmaringen ～ pass the city's waste-water treatment plant ～ and ride between the edge of the forest and the Danube towards Sigmaringendorf.

Sigmaringendorf

Postal Code: 72517; Area code: 07571

ℹ **Mayor's office**, ☏ 73050

🏛 **Bruck Chapel**

Sigmaringen

6

Kugelberg
275

Unterschmeien

Kitzisberg
750

Brenzkofer Berg
660

Mattes-Zündapp-Museum

Bootshaus

Sigmaringen

Gutensteiner Berg Schmeirer Berg
710   655

Teufelsloch

5,5

Sigmaringen Palace

Hedinger Church

15

Neugutenstein Ruin

Nickhof

Inzigkofer Park

Laiz

Dietfurt Dietfurt

St. Peter und Paul

4,5

Amalien rock

Känzele
Abbey Museum
Former Abbey Church

Teufelsbrücke

14

Henselmann Museum

3,5

Donau

13

stein

Benzenberg
.720

Geizenbühl
.695

Inzigkofen

Agricultural Museum

Kappenbühl
625

Bruck Cha

7

Alter Berg
710

Neuberg
710

Vilsingen

Alleeberg
655

Josefslust

33

Sonderhartbühl

Pault

After the Danube bridge take the moderately-busy **L 455** local road ~ at the next intersection turn left ~ and proceed on the unpaved track along the Danube ~ riding between the woods and the river towards Scheer ~ the track becomes narrow as you enter the town ~ and widens again after the railway underpass ~ the route makes a loop through the part of the town which lies on the inside of the river bend.

Roman Museum Ennetach

Scheer

Postal Code: 72516; Area code: 07572

- 🛈 **Mayor's office**, ☎ 76160
- 🏰 **Grafenschloss** (1485-1496)
- 🏰 **Bartelstein Palace**, 16th c. palace rebuilt in the 17th c., its name is derived from a site of public executions. Private.
- ⛪ **St. Nikolaus church**, built as a gothic, triple-nave basilica in the 14th c., renovated in Rococo style in the 18th c. Interior with stucco and fresco decorations.

The small town of Scheer lies at the eastern end of the upper Danube valley. This is where the river leaves the Swabian Alb and enters a wider valley. The city's historic structures include the renaissance palace and the Bartelstein palace, and testify to the 700-year history of Scheer and the Grafschaft Friedberg-Scheer.

16 Keep right across the railway line before reaching the railway sation ~ follow the street along the right side of the railway line to Enntach.

Ennetach (see also Mengen)

Postal Code: 88512; Area code: 07572

- 🏛 **Roman Museum**, Kastellstr. 52, ☎ 769504, Open: Mar.-Nov., Tue-Sun 10-18.
- ✱ **Gaggli Nudelhouse**, Mühlstr. 8-10, Enntach, ☎ 759440, Open: Guided tours Tue-Thur 10 am & Tue-Wed 2 pm, registration required. View noodle production from the mixing of the first ingredients to final packaging.

Turn right at the T-intersection with the **Scheerer Straße** ~ in the bend in front of the **Römermuseum** (Roman museum) ride straight ahead into **Mühlstraße** ~ pass the Gaggli Nudel House ~ after crossing the railway tracks, keep left through the underpass ~ turn right ~ and pass the outdoor pool ~ after the small bridge turn left onto **Mühlgassle** ~ follow the right bend, then turn left onto the **Hauptstraße** in Mengen.

Mengen

Postal Code: 88512; Area code: 07572

- 🛈 **Tourist-Info Mengen**, Bürgerbüro Mengen, Hauptstr. 90, ☎ 6070, www.mengen.de.
- 🏰 **Lookout Tower** on the Missionsberg

Lauercherthal

Schöchen
655

Scheer

Belren

N

Beurener Brücke

2,5

Grafenschloss

Sigmaringendorf

Blochingen

Donau

16

Bruck Chapel

Berg
605

4

L268

5,7

17

Hipfelsberg
4,5

B32

Ennetach

Mengen

B32

Roman Museum

Gaggli Nudelhouse

Parish Church

Haupstraße

Käserne Mengen

Waldhof

Missionsberg
695

L283

Waldberg
675

Zielfingen

Zielfinger See

B311

35

Beizkofen

Sudsee

Ostrach

Mengen, view from the Missionsberg

- ✷ Impressive medieval historic centre.
- 🏖 Zielfinger See, bathing lake southwest of Mengen, with beach and restaurants.
- 🚲 Zweiradcenter Bacher GbR, Mittlere Str. 33, ☎ 5696

The old city centre of Mengen contains numerous well-preserved half-timbered houses. A written guide is available for a short tour or one can join guided groups to learn more about the city's history. Artifacts from region's Hallstatt and Roman past have been found throughout the region and can be seen at the award-winning Mengen-Ennetach Römermuseum which reopened in July 2001. It stands directly on the Danube hiking trail and also features a multi-media

presentation that provides insights into life in Roman times. Mengen acquired city status under the Staufers before becoming a possession of the Habsburgs. In 1276 it obtained the same rights and freedoms as the city of Freiburg im Breisgau. Mengen was one of the five so-called Eastern Austrian Danube cities until 1806, when it became part of Württemberg.

Mengen to Riedlingen   17.8 km

Continue along the **Hauptstraße** ～ go straight at the two roundabouts by the railway station, where the street becomes the **Riedlinger Straße** ～ a bicycle path begins here on the left side of the street ～ continue below the railway line and a road bridge ～ on the **Blochinger Straße** straight at the roundabout ～ **17** turn right just before the bridge over the Danube ～ keep left at the first fork, then right at the second ～ follow the paved lane until you reach a bridge over the Danube.

ALTERNATIVE Here you have the option of continuing straight ahead to enjoy the fabulous views into the Danube valley from the heights

along the Beuren-Hundersingen road on the way to Hundersingen. From there you can continue to Binzwangen, passing the Heuneburg Museum and open-air museum Heuneburg on the way. The route is given in orange on map 8.

Herbertingen-Hundersingen
Postal Code: 88518; Area code: 07586

- ℹ️ Local Council, Holzg. 6, Herbertingen, ☎ 92080
- 🏛 Heuneburg Museum and open-air museum Keltischer Fürstensitz Heuneburg, Binzwanger Str. 14 and 2 km from Hundersingen towards Binzwangen, ☎ 1679, Open: Apr.-Oct., Tue-Sun/Hol. 10-17. Exhibits of early Celtic finds (600-400 BC) from the nearby Heuneburg, where an open-air museum brings the settlement to life through numerous reconstructions. Archaeological hiking trail to one of the largest celtic burial mounds in central Europe.

Keltischer Fürstensitz Heuneburg

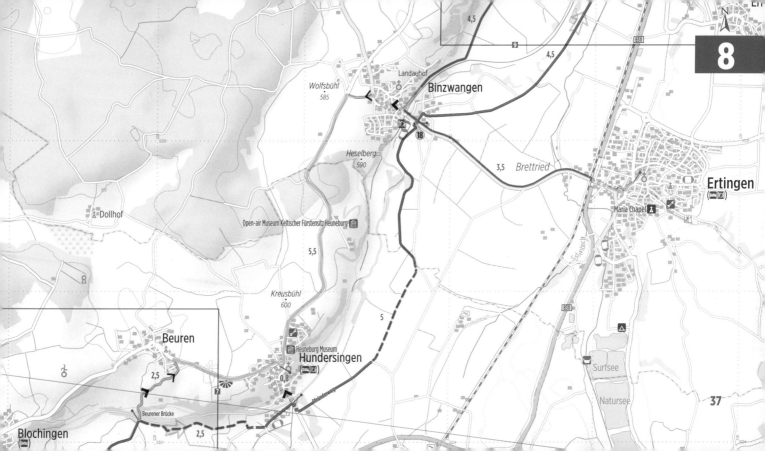

N

8

4,5

9

4,5

B311

Landauhof

Wolfsbühl
585

Binzwangen

4,5

18

Heselberg
590

3,5   Brettried

Ertingen

Open-air Museum Keltischer Fürstensitz Heuneburg

Dollhof

Maria Chapel

5,5

Kreusbühl
600

5

Beuren

B311

Heuneburg Museum

Hundersingen

Surfsee

2,5

0,8

37

Natursee

Beurener Brücke

Blochingen   2,5

🚲 **Hinderhofer Landmaschinen**, Binzwanger Str. 24, ☎ 203

To stay on the main route, turn right in front of the bridge into the unpaved field road ∼ keep left ∼ then left again onto **Mühlenweg** ∼ turn right when you reach the main road (K 8261) from Hundersingen ∼ turn left after a short distance onto a small, paved road ∼ ride straight ahead in the right bend ∼ follow the field road all the way to the **L 278** after the playing fields in Binzwangen **18**.

EXCURSION Here you have the option of a short excursion to Ertingen about 3.5 km distant.

Ertingen

Postal Code: 88521; Area code: 07371

🏛 **Mayor's office**, Dürmentinger Str. 14, ☎ 5080

🏠 **Michel-Buck-Stube**

⛪ **Maria Chapel** from 1693 (with ceiling paintings by J.- I. Wegscheider)

✉ **Recreation centre** "Schwarzachtalseen".

🚲 **Velorado Echsle**, Im Stillen Grund 13, ☎ 5702

Binzwangen

ALTERNATIVE There are attractive and well-marked bicycle routes on both sides of the Danube between Binzwangen and Riedlingen. You can choose from either the direct route on the right bank or the somewhat longer route via Altheim on the left bank. The left bank route has the advantage of being paved the entire way.

Left bank alternative via Altheim   *8.5 km*

Turn left onto the bicycle path along the L 278 ∼ turn right into the side street immediately after the bridge ∼ after 300 m it becomes a bicycle path and later a field road ∼ keep left then right at the two thee-way intersections by Waldhausen ∼ turn right at the T-intersection ∼ left after 200 m.

EXCURSION After another 250 m there is a turnoff to Neufra on the other bank of the Danube.

Continue along the paved field road, which becomes the **Donaustraße** in Altheim.

Altheim

In Altheim turn right into the **Sandgrubenweg** ∼ turn right in the left curve and continue into the paved bicycle path ∼ turn left as you reach the river once more ∼ keep right as you reach Riedlingen ∼ turn left into the small lane beside the river ∼ cross the old bridge and continue to the T-intersection ∼ turn right and cross the bridge over the Danube canal ∼ turn left immediately after the bridge, which takes you back onto the main route along the paved bicycle path beside the canal.

Riedlingen

To continue along the right bank from Binzwangen, **18** proceed straight across the L 278 into

Neufra Palace

an industry and commerce zone ⁓ after 200 m turn right and take the small street towards Neufra ⁓ **19** after 4.5 km turn left at the T-intersection and proceed to the Danube.

EXCURSION At this T-intersection you can also turn right and visit the palace at Neufra, which is about 1.5 km distant.

Neufra

🦽 ♿ **Neufra Hanging Gardens**, Open: Apr.-Oct., Tue-Sun 10:30-18.

The "hanging garden" is one special attraction of the Neufra palace. The former renaissance garden built on 16-meters tall support walls by Count Georg von Helfenstein between 1569 and 1573 has been redesigned and opened to the public. It also offers fine views into the Danube valley.

After 150 m turn right on the gravel bicycle path ⁓ at first beside the Danube, you come to ride beside the Danube canal ⁓ after 2.5 km you arrive in Riedlingen.

CENTRE The centre of Riedlingen lies across the river to the left.

Riedlingen

Postal Code: 88499; Area code: 07371

🛈 **Information** in the town hall, Marktpl. 1, ✆ 1830, www.riedlingen.de

🏛 **Museum "Schöne Stiege"** Rössleg. 1, ✆ 909633, Open: Apr.-8th Dec., Fri, Sat 15-17, Sun 14-17 and additional exhibition spaces in the **"Spital zum Hl. Geist"**, Am Wochenmarkt 3.

🦽 **Catholic parish church St. Georg**, late-gothic 15th c. church noteworthy especially for its baptismal chapel.

❊ **Wegscheider House**, decorated in the 18th c. by the well-known Riedlingen painter Josef Ignaz Wegscheider.

❊ **Rathaus (Town Hall)**, The gothic style town hall with two steeples is the most noteworthy building in Riedlingen.

🚲 **Radsport Günzel**, Unterriedstr. 15, ✆ 927298

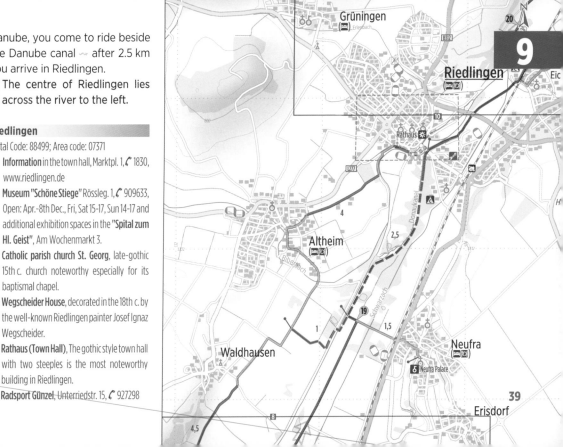

The settlement of Riedlingen dates back to lands owned by Louis I (Louis the Pious, or Ludwig der Fromme in German) from the year 835. Between 1247 and 1255 the Counts of Veringen founded a typical new city east of the original settlement with streets laid out at right angles. The main street became the market square.

In the 14th century town residents then enlarged their city by adding the original hamlet and extending the city's area down to the Danube. Its location at the intersection of the river with the main road helped the town to grow. Its prosperity is reflected by the impressive town hall, the city walls and the elaborate half-timbered houses. Riedlingen is in one of the few communities in the region that managed to mostly avoid the devastation brought by war and plundering armies during Europe's most violent periods.

A tour through the old town starts at the town hall, a distinctive structure with stepped gables built in 1447 as a storehouse for grain and goods. On the roof there is a stork's nest that attracts a family of the great migrating birds every summer. Across the market square one comes to the "Alte Kaserne" on Apothekergasse, a granary from 1686. Next stop is the house with the "Schönen Stiege", which today holds the town museum. Across from it, the "Altes Spital". Through the city gate one comes to the moat along the city wall and the cemetery that belonged to the former Kapuzinerkloster. The church "Spitalkirche" contains works by the famous Riedlingen artists J. J. Christian and Johann de Pay.

Cross Hospitalstraße and Gammertinger Straße to reach the old Weilervorstadt part of town, with the baroque Weiler chapel from 1721, which was built to honor 14 holy "Nothelfer," or helpers in times of need, a group of saints who provide help or solace in times of crisis. Images of the group can be found in many church paintings made after the 14th century. Returning to the town hall one passes the Wegscheider Haus on Lange Straße. It is a baroque city palace from 1742 which today contains the city library. Finally, one should pass through the small park behind the town hall, where the Zwiefalter Gate and the Zellemess tower of the city wall can be found.

Riedlingen to Munderkingen   24.7 km

After crossing the road, continue along the bicycle path beside the canal out of Riedlingen ～ you pass under the main road ～ and reach **Vöhringer Hof** after crossing a small bridge.

TIP

Here the Donau-Bodensee (Danube-Lake Constance) bicycle route forks off to the right over the railway tracks.

Keep left of the tracks ~ **20** past the wastewater treatment plant ~ and along the lane towards Daugendorf.

Riedlingen

Daugendorf

At the intersection in Daugendorf turn left across the bridge ~ turn right immediately after the bridge ~ at the intersection in the fields, turn right and proceed to Bechingen ~ before the houses keep right then left and ride to the main street.

Bechingen

21 In Bechingen turn right onto the bicycle path along the K 7545 ~ cross the Danube just before Zell and stay on the K 7545 through Zell.

Zell

Turn left immediately after the bridge over the railway tracks ~ follow the lane beside the railway tracks to the railway bridge, which you use to cross the river ~ after another 500 m turn left across the tracks and follow the street into Zwiefaltendorf.

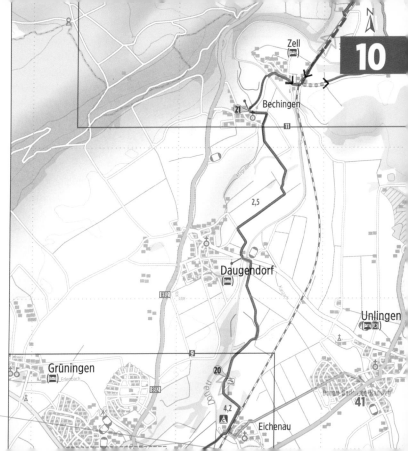

10

Zell

Bechingen

21

Daugendorf

Unlingen

Grüningen

Eichenau

41

2,5

9

4,2

20

Danube by Obermarchtal

Zwiefaltendorf

EXCURSION From here you can make a side-trip to Zwiefalten and the interesting Benedictine abbey. The town is several kilometers to the west and can be reached on a bicycle path along the left side of the Zwiefacher Ach creek.

Zwiefalten excursion   6 km

In Zwiefaltendorf turn left before Hauptstraße and head to the stream on the right ～ follow it on the left side up to Zwiefalten.

Zwiefalten

Postal Code: 88529; Area code: 07373

ℹ️ Touristinformation, in the town hall, Marktpl. 3, ✆ 20520

🏛 Former Benedictine abbey and Minster, ✆ 2252, Minster open: summer daily 9:30-18, winter Mon-Sat 10-16, Sun 9:30-16. The former abbey now houses a psychiatric clinic. The Minster is one of the most important German late-Baroque buildings, constructed by Johann Michael Fischer 1739-65.

The former Benedictine abbey at Zwiefalten contains rich examples of late baroque and rococo church art.

Return to Zwiefaltendorf by the same route. In Zwiefaltendorf turn right on the L 271 ～ cross the Danube and turn left on the gravel path before the railway crossing ～ ride along the tracks ～ after crossing the tracks the road climbs steeply up to Datthausen ～ ride out to the B 311 main road.

Datthausen

After crossing the busy road, turn left onto the paved lane which runs beside the B 311 ～ continue through the underpass and keep left up to the T-intersection **22**.

FORK Here you have two possibilities for continuing: The longer main route to the left takes you through Rechtenstein, with its imposing castle, while the alternative route to the right bypasses Rechtenstein, taking you directly to Obermarchtal and the noteworthy abbey church, which can also be easily reached from the main route.

Via Obermarchtal   5.5 km

Turn right at the T-intersection and follow the paved field road beside the B 311 to Obermarchtal ～ keep left onto the main street ～ turn right into the first side street to continue on the **Sebastian-Sailer-Straße** ～ ride 200 m to the centre of the town.

FORK Turn left here if you want to visit the Abbey or take the connection to the main route along the river.

Obermarchtal

Postal Code: 89611; Area code: 07375

ℹ️ **Mayors office**, Hauptstr. 21, ✆ 205

🏛 **Obermarchtal Abbey church**, designated a minster in 2001, guided tours: ✆ 959100. Former Premonstratensian monastery is the oldest baroque church in upper Swabia. Contains important artworks and stucco work in the refectory and mirrored chamber.

✳️ **Soldiers' cemetery**, also called the "Strangers' cemetery" because many travelers, pilgrims and soldiers have been buried here since 1790.

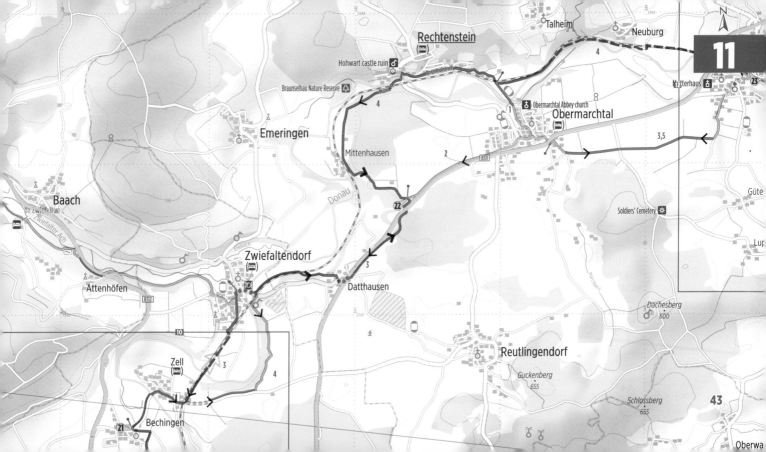

11

Talheim

Neuburg

Rechtenstein

Hohwart castle ruin

Braunhofstraße

Mühle

23

Ritterhaus

Braunselhau Nature Reserve

4

Obermarchtal Abbey church

Obermarchtal

3,5

Emeringen

Mittenhausen

Donau

2

B311

Güte

Soldiers' Cemetery

Lur

22

Baach

to Zwiefalten

Zwiefalter Ach

Ebisbach

Zwiefaltendorf

3

Datthausen

Dachesberg
600

Attenhöfen

B312

Reutlingendorf

10

Zell

3

4

Guckenberg
655

Schlossberg
655

43

21

Bechingen

Oberwa

The former Premonstratensian monastery in Obermarchtal contains some of the most beautiful examples of German baroque stucco church decorations of the Wessobrunner school. Marie Antoinette, the youngest daughter of Empress Maria, stayed here on her way to Paris. In the early 19th century the monastery was closed and the grounds were turned over to the Counts of Thurn und Taxis. Since 1973 it has been the property of the Rottenburg-Stuttgart diocese.

To continue on the alternative route to Untermarchtal, ride straight ahead ∿ after a short distance on the **Hauptstraße** turn right into the **Oberwachinger Str.** ∿ after passing under the main road, turn left ∿ follow the right bend along the small street ∿ turn left at the intersection in the fields ∿ follow the paved road ∿ at the next intersection continue straight ahead into the field road ∿ turn left at the T-intersection ∿ follow the paved lane through a small wooded ravine down to Untermarchtal.

22 To follow the main route via Rechtenstein, turn left at the T-intersection and follow the paved lane down into the valley ∿ pass Mittenhausen ∿ after passing through a forest you cross the railway line ∿ turn left at the T-intersection with the L 249 ∿ cross the Danube and turn right when you reach Rechtenstein.

Rechtenstein

Postal Code: 89611; Area code: 07375

🛈 **Mayor's office**, Braunselweg 2, ☎ 244

🏰 Hohwart castle ruin

Obermarchtal and its lush surroundings are visible from the lookout point from the ruins of Hohwart in Rechtenstein.

The 12th century Burg Hohwart has been a ruin since the early 18th century. This picturesque

Rechtenstein

bend in the Danube also has the Brauselhau nature preserve with its old creeks and protruding cliffs. The Schelmental and its bizarre rock formations are a short hike away.

Keep left at the fork ∿ turn right into **Brühlhofstraße** ∿ follow this street out of Rechtenstein ∿ after the railway crossing turn left onto a paved bicycle path, which turns to gravel after about 100 meters.

EXCURSION To reach Obermarchtal, simply continue straight after the railway crossing.

Ride through the nature reserve where the Lauter stream enters the Danube ∿ after the rock outcrops by Neuburg the path takes you left across the railway line ∿ immediately turn right and follow the field road along the railway line ∿ continue on the paved lane under the road bridge into Untermarchtal.

Untermarchtal

Postal Code: 89617; Area code: 07393

🛈 **Infozentrum**, Bahnhofstr. 4, ☎ 917383

🏛 World's First **Broom Museum**, Schloss Mochental, ☎ 07395/418, Open: Tue-Sat 13-17, Sun/Hol. 11-17.

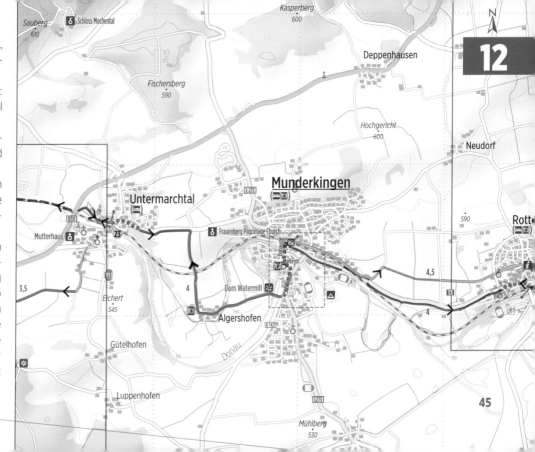

- 🏛 **Kalkofenmuseum (lime kiln museum)**, ✆917383, Open: Apr.-Oct., Sun/Hol 11-17. Operated between 1922 and 1939 and still in operational condition.
- 🏛 **Galerie Ewald Karl Schrade**, Schloss Mochental, ✆ 07395/418, Open: Tue-Sat 13-17, Sun/Hol. 11-17. Changing exhibitions, from classical modernism to contemporary art.
- 🏰 **Schloss Mochental**, north of Untermarchtal, the Renaissance-style palace from the 18th c. overlooks the Danube valley and houses a gallery and broom museum.
- ⛪ **Untermarchtal convent (Mutterhaus)**, the former palace from 1576 has served as a convent of the Sisters of Mercy since the late 19th c. The grounds of the complex can be explored on foot provided one is quiet.

Follow the street to the T-intersection ⤳ **23** turn left onto the busy L 257 ⤳ as you leave Untermarchtal, ride onto the paved field road along the right side of the **L 257** ⤳ after a slight climb turn right towards Algershofen ⤳ ride through **Algershofen** and take the tree-lined avenue towards Munderkingen ⤳ after crossing the Danube, keep left at both intersections ⤳ follow the main street past the cemetery ⤳ turn left into **Martinstraße** ⤳ left into Kirchgasse.

12

Munderkingen

Postal Code: 89597; Area code: 07393

🛈 **Town hall**, Marktstr. 1, ☎ 5980, www.munderkingen.de

🏛 **Town Museum**, in the former Holy Spirit hospital, Schulhof 1, ☎ 1568, Open: Apr.-Oct, Sun 14-17 and by appt. Local excavations, life during Roman and Alemannic times (bronze statues), city and church history, brush making, dolls and dolls-houses.

🛐 **St. Dionysius parish church**. Gothich church with Renaissance and Baroque elements. Panel paintings by the Master of the Munderking Altar.

❋ **Dom watermill**, Algershofer Weg 4, Tours by arrangement with Josef Dom ☎ 1305, Open: Mon-Sat 8-12:15, Mon, Tue, Thur, Fri also 14-18. Shop.

❋ **Historic city centre,** with town hall, half-timbered houses and three renaissance fountains.

Munderkingen was one of the Habsburg possessions west of Austria. The picturesque old city with its many gabled roofs, churches and narrow streets is surrounded on three sides by the Danube, which makes a tight loop around the city.

Munderkingen to Ehingen   13,1 km

Beside St. Dionysius church turn right into the narrow lane ᷈ continue straight into **Donaustraße** and over the bridge across the Danube ᷈ turn right onto the bicycle path along the **L 257** ᷈ cross the intersection with **Angerweg** ᷈ after 500 m the path changes to the other side of the street ᷈ after the railway crossing, follow the bicycle path across the side street and back to the right side of the **L 257**.

Rottenacker

In Rottenacker the bike path ends at the church ᷈ ride on the main street through the village.

Rottenacker

Postal Code: 89616; Area code: 07393

🛈 **Mayor's office**, Bühlstr. 7, ☎ 95040, www.rottenacker.de

🏛 **Local history museum "Wirtles Haus"**, Open: May-Oct., 1st and 3rd Sun each month 14-17 and by appt. Guided tours: ☎ 95040. Folk crafts, life on the Danube and much more.

❋ Award winning **city centre** (awarded twice in 2005)

✉ Lake **Heppenäcker**, SE of town, beautifully situated lake with amenities and a kiosk.

🚲 **Zweirad Lerner**, Grundlerstr. 2, ☎ 2509

Ride onto the bridge over the railway line ᷈ turn left into **Bahnhofstraße** (L 255) before crossing the river ᷈ **24** after 100 m turn right onto the old pedestrian and bicycle bridge across the Danube ᷈ turn left on the bike path on **Kirchbierlinger Straße** (L 257) ᷈ after one kilometre turn left ᷈ keep right after the wastewater treatment plant and continue towards Dettingen ᷈ keep right by the first bridge over the Danube ᷈ continue between fields over the bridge into Dettingen.

Dettingen

Over the tracks ⌁ **25** turn right onto bicycle path along the **L 255** ⌁ at the intersection, keep left and continue on the path along the left side of the **B 465** main road ⌁ after 2 km cross the B 465 at the pedestrian light by the **Schwarze Gasse** and follow the signs to the **Marktplatz** in Ehingen.

You are now standing on Ehingen's large market with its original market fountain. The handsome old merchant houses and the city wall testify to the city's rich history.

Ehingen

Postal Code: 89584; Area code: 07391

- 🛈 **Tourist Info**, Marktpl. 1, ✆ 503-216 or 207, www.ehingen.de
- 🏛 **Museum Ehingen** and **Spitalkapelle** (Hospital Chapel), in the former Heilig-Geist-Spital, Am Viehmarkt, ✆ 503-531; Open: Wed 10-12 & 14-17, Sat, Sun 14-17, Tours by appt. Secular and religious art, folk art and culture, exotic animals.

The late gothic chapel houses impressive wall paintings.

- 🏛 **Städtische Galerie (Town gallery)**, Tränkberg 9, ✆ 503-500, Open: Sat, Sun 14-17. Modern art and the Doris Nöth collection.
- 🕇 **St.Blasius parish church**, 14th c. church with Baroque elements.
- 🕇 Baroque **Liebfrauenkirche (Church of our lady)** and Former **Franciscan Monastery** (17th c.)
- 🕇 **Sacred Heart church** and former **Benedictine college**
- ✺ **Market square** with Ständehaus (regional adminitration building), **fountain**, former **knights house**
- ✺ **Wolfert tower, city wall**
- ✺ **City tours** by appointment, ✆ 75065 or 503531
- ✺ **Ehinger Musiksommer**, June-July, Open Air **Filmfestival**, Aug., **Ehinger Jazz days**, Oct., further information at the Tourist Info.
- ✺ **Ehinger cycle tours**, **Museum Tour** and **Ecology Tours**, further information at the Tourist Info.
- ✉ **Heated outdoor pool**, by the Donauhalde.
- 🚲 **Radgarage**, Biberacher Str. 4, ✆ 52483
- 🚲 **Rad+Sport Ersing**, Hauptstr. 195, ✆ 7819642

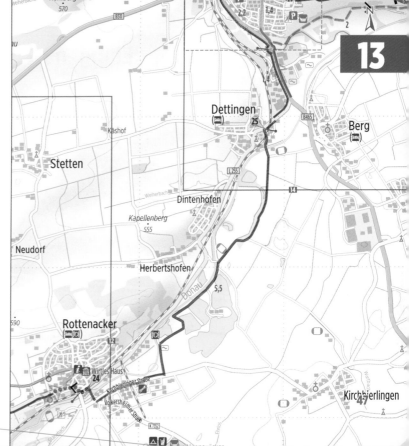

13

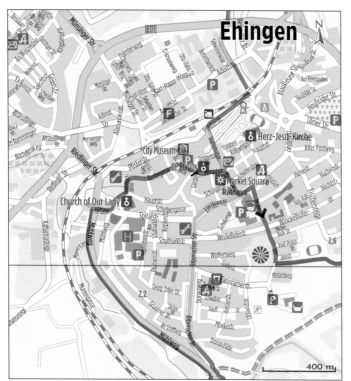

Ehingen

B311

Herz-Jesu-Kirche

City Museum
St. Blasius
Market Square
Rathaus

Church of Our Lady

2,6

2,2

400 m

Franciscan Monastery Ehingen

Radsport Bott, Funkenweg 8, ☏ 752191

ALTERNATIVE

In Ehingen you faced with a tough choice. Either you stay on the main route along the Danube to Ulm or you take an alternative route through the idyllic (Blautal) Blau valley to Blaubeuren and the famous Blautopf.

Blautal alternative   42.5 km

Ehingen to Blaubeuren   21 km

TIP

The Blautal alternative begins at the Marktplatz in Ehingen. The route is posted with signs that say Donau Radweg, Alternative Blautal and leads first to the train station.

In front of the train station go right ～ and ride along the left side of the street ～ in the curve turn left ～ go under the railroad bridge ～ and along the stream and under the Bundesstraße ～ turn left on **Rosenstraße** ～ the next town is **Berkach** ～ turn right on **Allmendinger Straße** and then continue straight ahead ～ on the quiet road towards Allmendingen.

Allmendingen

Postal Code: 89604, Area code: 07391

ℹ️ **Council office**, Hauptstr. 16, ✆ 70150

Follow **Kleindorfer Straße** ∿ turn left on **Katzensteige** before you come to the railroad crossing ∿ and turn right on the next right-of-way street and then immediately left ∿ and follow the road toward **Schmiechen** ∿ take the road right into Schmiechen ∿ and turn right on K 7408 ∿ and then the bike path along the left side of the B 492 ∿ to the left towards Schelklingen.

Schelklingen

✱ **Stone age cave "Hohler Fels"**, ✆ 07394/595 or 2685 or 916766. Tours Sundays after 2pm or by appointment.

As you enter town turn right ∿ and follow the road through newly built area ∿ continue right

Deep Blue of the Blautopf

straight across the L 240 and into a dead-end street ∿ at the end of the dead-end street continue straight ahead ∿ cross the B 492 at the pedestrian crossing light ∿ ride past the Gasthof Hohler Felsen ∿ under the railroad ∿ and past the open-air pool and the stone-age cave "Hohler Fels".

At the next intersection stay left ∿ turn right before you cross the railroad tracks and proceed towards **Weiler** ∿ at the first houses go over the bridge and keep right

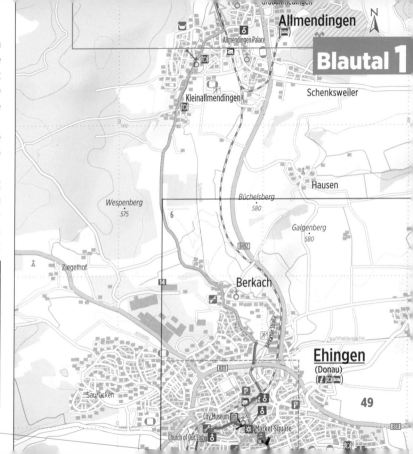

49

Hohle Fels
Hohler Fels Cave

Schelklingen

Hilzbe..
460

Schneckenburren
460

Schmiechen

Schelkinger Berg
685

Egelsberg
685

B492

Lake Schmiechen

Erzberg
630

Steinsberg
645

1

50

Großallmedingen

Allmendingen

Allmendingen Palace

~ cross the main road straight into the village ~ immediately turn right on **Wiesenweg** ~ turn right again into the **Wiesenweg**, which becomes a bike path ~ continue on the bicycle path along the main road into Blaubeuren.

Blaubeuren

Postal Code: 89143, Area code: 07344

🅹 **Tourism office**, Aachg. 7, ☎ 921025 or 96690, www.blaubeuren.de

🏛 **Urgeschichtliches Museum (Prehistory museum)**, Karlstr. 21, ☎ 9286-0, Open: 15th Mar.-Nov., Tue-Sun 10-17, Dec.-14th Mar., Tue, Sat 14-17, Sun 10-17.

🏛 **Schubartstube**, in the former deanery of the Blaubeuren monastery, Info: ☎ 962625, Open: by appt. Literary memorial to the poets Ch. F. D. Schubart, Eduard Mörike and Agnes Sapper.

🔔 **Benedictine monastery**, founded around 1100. The monastery church, built 1491-99, holds many late 15th century artworks from the Ulm school.

✳ **Guided city tours**, meet Saturdays at 10:30 at the info point. Groups should call in advance; tannery quarter on the Ach with remains of the city walls.

✳ **Blautopf**, legendery source of the Blau river. About 2,000 liters per second bubble to the surface from a depth of 20 m; historic **hammer mill** and cave research centre.

✳ **Monks bathhouse** (built 1510)

✉ **heated outdoor pool**

🛏 **Indoor swimming pool**

🚲 🚲 **Rund ums Rad Käppeler**, Karlstr. 52, ☎ 6398

The old smithy at the Blautopf, Blaubeuren

Blautal 3
Beurer Berg
660
Seißen
B28
Blautopf
Benedictine monastery
Blaubeuren
Sonderbuch
Karlstraße
Blau
Buckenberg
Frauenberg
550
Brillen Cave
7,5
Weiler
Gerhausen
B28
Blau
B492
8
Oberschelkingen
Dietir
Hintere Gleißenburg
Markbr
Schlossberg
685
Hohenschelklingen Castle
Vordere Gleißenburg
Höhe
685
Beiningen
Geißenkopf
670
Hohle Fels
Hohler Fels Cave
Schelklingen
Ziegelhofen

Use the traffic light at the main intersection to cross the B 28 ～ this puts you on **Weilerstraße** ～ go through the curve and then straight ～ turn right after 800 m ～ turn left on **Karlstraße** ～ continue along the **Klosterstraße** ～ turn right into **Blautopfstraße** and you soon reach the Blautopf spring.

The Blautopf is an impressive large karst spring. Its extensive system of caves beneath the mountain have been explored to a depth of more than 1,200 meters.

Blaubeuren to Ulm   21.5 km

To continue the tour stay on the same road ～ it comes to a fork ～ take **Mühlweg** which leads downhill ～ follow the signs to the other side of the river ～ turn left directly in front of the indoor pool ～ and follow the street through the curve to the right ～ then turn left on a bike and pedestrian path along the Blau towards Gerhausen.

Gerhausen

In Gerhausen ride a short distance on the left side of Hauptstraße ～ then turn right on **Unter**

dem Schillerstein ～ turn left at the next right-of-way street ～ and then right at the factory building ～ then left on **Gartenstraße** ～ and immediately right again ～ and then right before the bridge over the Blau ～ ride along the right side of the Blau ～ and stay on the valley floor ～ at first the path is paved with asphalt ～ after the Hohenstein there's a short stretch of gravel.

Arnegg

Just as you enter Arnegg turn left on **Oberer Wiesenweg** ～ after a curve to the right turn left on the main road ～ and proceed straight on the L 1244 through the village until the bicycle route goes off the road to the left ～ take the unpaved track to Blaustein.

Blaustein

Postal Code: 89134, Area code: 07304

🛈 **Town office**, Marktpl. 2, ✆ 8020

🛁 **Bad Blau** with sauna village and outdoor brine tubs

🚲 **Radsport Pfister**, Max-Hilsenbeck-Str. 7, ✆ 42192

Blaustein is just outside Ulm where the Swabian Alb and Upper Swabia meet. Ulm is known for its university and cathedral and lies in a landscape of large forests and juniper heaths.

Klingenstein

As you near the edge of Klingenstein turn left over the bridge across the Blau ～ turn right after crossing the railway tracks ～ at the T-intersection turn right and immediately left into **Ehrensteiner Straße** ～ take the second left into **Josefweg** ～ at the end of the street keep right and follow the bicycle path along the river ～ continuen along the river, crossing three streets along the way ～ after the third street you come to follow a lane along the railway tracks ～ after passing under the bridge of the K 9915 keep right ～ follow the bicycle path under the railway bridge and along the river ～ at the T-intersection keep left ～ turn right through the underpass under the K 9903 and immediately right again under the B 28 ～ once again along the course of the Blau ～ turn right at **Magirusstraße** ～ turn left into the bicycle path immediately after the bridge over the Blau ～ turn left over the small bridge across the river and immediately right ～ follow the bicycle path along the stream ～ after passing under the B 10 turn right onto the two-lane

bicycle path ∿ you ride parallel to the B 10 ∿ at **Ehinger Tor** turn left on the bike path on **Neue Straße** ∿ after passing under a railway underpass turn left before the next underpass ∿ follow the loop of the bicycle path up the railway tracks ∿ follow the path along the tracks and under a road bridge ∿ continue straight to the river, where you turn left onto the main route into the centre of Ulm.

Ulm (refer to page 58)

Ehingen to Ulm 32.5 km

Leave the market in Ehingen along the **Marktstraße** ∿ turn left on **Lindenstraße** ∿ immediately turn right on **Müllerstraße** ∿ at the end of the climb turn left on the bicycle path ∿ you get a nice view into the Danube valley as you pass the playing fields ∿ turn right as you reach a street, the **Gollenäcker** ∿ turn right again into the first side street and follow the right bend onto **Kapellenstraße**.

Nasgenstadt

Follow this street between the houses all the way to the L 259 ∿ turn right and ride on the bicycle path along the **L 259** ∿ by Griesingen the path crosses the main road.

Griesingen

Turn left at the intersection with the small road ∿ turn right into the paved field road ∿ at the T-intersection turn left and ride toward Öpfingen.

Öpfingen

Postal Code: 89614; Area code: 07391

🛈 **Mayor's office**, Schlosshofstr. 10, ✆ 7084-0

As you reach the first houses, cross the road and take the side street to the right ∿ continue straight along the field road 4.5 km to Ersingen ∿ turn left at the T-intersection onto **Rißtisser Straße** ∿ in the left bend, turn right into **Mittelstraße**.

Ersingen

Postal Code: 89155; Area code: 07305

🛈 **Local administration**, Mittelstr. 11/1, ✆ 9262880

✉ **Bathing lake**

Gasthaus Hirsch & Campsite

• Located directly on the Danube bike trail, we offer an ideal place for cyclists to enjoy a meal and take a rest • the rural idyll which you find here will be an unforgettable experience, especially for your children.

26 Turn right by the church ∿ immediately left on **Seestraße** ∿ continue straight ahead onto the path ∿ turn left on the street between the playing fields ∿ cross the main road and ride to the right on the paved lane ∿ after 200 m turn left and follow the lane to the barrage on the Danube ∿ from here you follow the paved path along the water towards Erbach.

Erbach

Postal Code: 89155; Area code: 07305

🛈 **City office**, Erlenbachstr. 50, ✆ 96760, www.erbach-donau.de

🏛 **Palace museum**, Schloss Erbach, ✆ 4646, Open: Apr.-Nov., Sun/Hol. 14-18.

✉ **Lake with beach**

Turn right under the railway tracks ∿ continue straight onto the street **Riedmühle** ∿ turn left and immediately right by the entrance to the mill ∿ you ride along the water and under a road bridge **27**.

FORK Those not wishing to ride via Erbach have the choice to take a shorter and much quieter alternative route to Donaustetten from here, following the narrow lake formed by the dam on the Danube Canal.

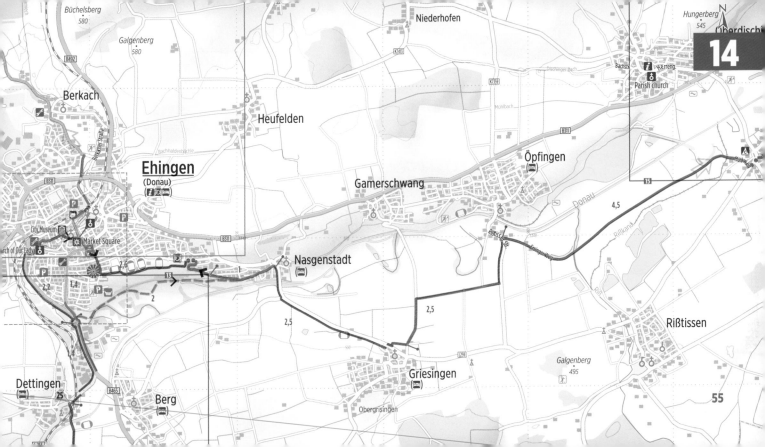

15

Hasenberg
540

N

Bach

Erbach
(E)

Erlenbach

Hagenbach

B311

Donaurieden

Schloss Erbach

Wilhelm-Blanck-Straße

Badesee

Riedmühle

27

4,7

Donau

Hungerberg
545

Oberdischingen

Herreng.

Parish church

14

56

26

Ersingen

Mühl

4

28

Gögglingen

1,8

16

Donaustetten

B30

2,4

1,2

Un

Umspannwerk Dellmensingen

Danube to Lake Constance

Rot

Riedtalstraße

Dellmensingen

Schulstraße

Lange Straße

Wassermühle

Weihergraben

Schammental

Weidengraben

Belzenberg
460

Humlangen

B30

Along the Danube canal   3.6 km

Continue straight ahead along the canal all the way to the powerstation on the dam ~ cross the dam and continue to the left along the water towards Donaustetten ~ after 300 m turn left onto the bicycle path along the L 240 and ride over the bridge across the Danube to rejoin the main route at **28**.

To follow the main route, **27** turn left immediately after passing under the bridge ~ follow the bicycle path along the K 7375 ~ when you reach the intersection, turn right onto the bicycle path along the **Heinrich-Hammer-Straße** ~ turn right after the tennis courts and follow the street **Großes Wert** ~ in the sharp left bend by the wastewater treatment plant turn right ~ follow the paved lane past ponds and along the Danube until you reach the **L 240** across the river from Donaustetten.

Donaustetten

28 cross the road and continue along the paved field road beside the Danube ~ by **Gögglingen** cross the **K 9916** and turn left along the bicycle

path ~ immediately turn right and continue on the path, at first along the Danube, then up to the street along the Donautal industrial zone ~ cross the street and turn right on the bicycle path along **Hans Lorenser Straße** ~ **29** turn right after the access road to the transformer station ~ you cross the Danube on a bicycle and pedestrian bridge through the Gronne nature reserve ~ turn left on the bike path along **Laupheimer Straße** ~ pass under the road bridge ~ turn left after 150 meters ~ turn right by the Danube and keep left at the fork in the path ~ follow the paved lane along the canal to the Wiblingen hydroelectric power station ~ cross the canal and the Danube and ride up to the railway line ~ turn right and follow the bicycle path along the railway line and the Danube towards Ulm ~ just after passing under a large road bridge you reach a small pedestrian and bicycle bridge.

ALTERNATIVE Here you have a choice of continuing on the Ulm side of the river or crossing over to Neu-Ulm on the south bank. On the north bank there are no streets to cross and the bicycle path

Ulm

is mostly separated from pedestrians. The route along the south bank bypasses Ulm, but offers terrific views of the old city and the cathedral. To stay on the main route towards the centre of Ulm, continue straight along the river bank ~ you pass below a railway bridge and pass along the historic town defences, behind which lies the magnificent historic centre of Ulm.

Ulm

Postal Code: 89073; Area code: 0731

🛈 **Tourist Information**, Münsterpl. 50, ✆ 1612830, www.tourismus.ulm.de

⚓ **Ship tours with the "Ulmer Spatz"**, from Metzgerturm, Information: R. Kräß, Augsburger Str. 96, ✆ 62751. Hourly river tours with the historic "Ulmer Spatz" from 1935 or with a solarpowered ferry or the larger steamer "MS Donau".

🏛 **Ulm Museum**, Marktpl. 9, ✆ 1614300 (Mon-Fri), ✆ 1614330 (Sat, Sun), Open: Tue-Sun 11-17, Thur 11-20. 20th c. art, Kurt Fried collection, late gothic, folk art and "Löwenmensch" archaeological collection.

🏛 **Weishaupt art gallery**, Hans- u. Sophie-Scholl-Pl. 1, ✆ 1614360, Open: Tue, Wed, Fri-Sun 11-17, Thur 11-20. Changing exhibitions in an interesting ambience.

🏛 **Bread Museum** in the Salzstadel, Salzstadelg. 10, ✆ 69955, Open: daily 10-17. History of bread and bread-making, unusual images of planting, harvest, eating, with a section on world food shortages.

🏛 **Haus der Stadtgeschichte**, Schwörhaus, Weinhof 12, ✆ 1614205, Open: Tue-Sun 11-17, free entry. City history.

🏛 **Nature education centre**, Kornhausg. 3, ✆ 1614742, Open: Tue-Fri 10-16, Sat, Sun 11-17. Of particular interest is part of a petrified palm trunk, the "Ulmer Palme"

🏛 **Donauschwäbisches central museum**, Schillerstr. 1, ✆ 962540, Open: Tue-Sun 11-17. History of Danube-Swabia presented within in impressive fortification walls.

🏛 **Edwin Scharff Museum**, Petruspl. 4, ✆ 70502555, Open: Tue, Wed 13-17, Thur-Sat 13-18, Sun 10-18. Museum of modern art and hands-on children's museum.

17

Lehr

B10

K9915

B19

Böfinger Halde

Pfuhler See

Wasserkraftwerk Böfinger Halde

Röhrensee

Botanik Gardens

Eselsberg

Safranberg
555

Ulm

Ulm Zoo

Pfuhl

Walther Collection

renstein

Wilhelmsburg Citadel

B19

B10

Friedrichsau

9   18

K9915

7,5

K9903

Roter Berg

Offenhausen

Söflingen Monastery

Gothic Cathedral

Neu-Ulm

Metzger Tower

St. John the Baptist

Wagnerstraße

0,6

Neue Str.

1

Söflingen

Römerstraße

Edwin-Scharff-Museum

B16

Burf

Donaubad Wonnemar

B28

B10

Concentration Camp Memorial

Egginger Weg

Schwaighofen

- ⑤ **Bundesfestung Ulm (Federal Fortifications)**, largest surviving 19th c. fortifications in Europe, built 1842-59. Guided tours year round by appointment at Tourist Information.
- ⑧ **Gothic cathedral (Münster)** with the world's tallest church tower (161.6 m), Open: daily 9-17, longer hours in summer.
- ⑧ **Wiblingen baroque monastery**, former Benedictine monastery with basilica and library, museum in the convent
- ✱ **Town hall (Rathaus)** with astronomical clock (1520)
- ✱ **Fisher and tanner quarter** at the mouth of the Blau
- ✱ other buildings of note include the **Schwörhaus, Zeughaus** (armory), **Schuhhaus** (former cobbler's guild house from 1537) and **Kornhaus** (former granary):
- ✱ **Historic city wall** along the Danube, with **Metzger tower**
- ✱ **Neue Mitte Ulm** with **Weishaupt art gallery, "Haus der Sinne," "Münstertor"** and **library**
- ✱ **Schwör week and water parades** "Nabada" (mid July)
- ✱ **Historic fisherman's day with parade**, light show on the Danube, international Danube festival
- ✱ **City tours**: 90 min. guided tours, Apr.-Oct., Mon-Sat 10 & 14:30, Sun/Hol 11:30 & 14:30, Nov.-Mar. Sat 10 & 14:30, Sun/Hol 11:30 & 14:30, starts at Tourist Information on the Münsterplatz (Stadthaus).
- ✱ **Kunstlandschaft Donau**, 7 km footpath between Adenauer bridge and Friedrichsau, both sides of the river, with about 45 large sculptures.

- ▢ **Ulm Zoo**, Friedrichsau 38, ✆ 1616742, Open: Apr.-Sept., daily 10-18, Oct.-Mar., daily 10-17.
- ▭ **Westbad**, Moltkestr. 30, ✆ 1613480
- ▨ 🚲 **Reich's Radl Shop**, Gideon-Bacher-Str. 3, ✆ 21179
- ▨ **Thürheimer Zweiradhandel**, Blaubeurer Str. 16, ✆ 176800
- ▨ **Bikeline-Ulm**, Sterng. 9, ✆ 6021358
- ▨ **Radladen am Karlsplatz**, Zeitblomstr. 31, ✆ 15975-34
- ▨ **Rad & Service**, Ochseng. 41b, ✆ 9386323
- 🚲 **Bicycle garage** and covered parking at the train station.

One of the prettiest parts of Ulm must surely be the fisher and tanner quarter - a dense neighborhood of old half-timbered houses that have settled with age and lean over the narrow streets and the waters of the Blau. It takes no great fantasy to imagine the smells and sounds as fishermen and merchants traded plump carp, pike and other fresh fish caught in the nearby Danube. Ulm's rivermen made an important contribution to the city's prosperity, using their famous Ulm-barges to transport goods and settlers from Swabia down the Danube. When these simple vessels arrived in Vienna, they were taken apart and sold as firewood because dragging them back upstream would have cost too much time and money. As with many other crafts, industrialization brought the end of that way of life. Today the picturesque streets and the quadrennial Fischerstechen serve as reminders of that past. The Fischerstechen is a jousting competition in which contestants try to push each other into the water.

A short distance downstream one comes to the tilted Metzger tower. According to local legend, the tower started to lean when local butchers met there to plot how they would deny accusations that they were making their sausages smaller and smaller.

Danube by Ulm

One tower that definitely does not lean is the tallest church steeple in the world: the soaring tower of Ulm's cathedral. It reaches 161.6 meters into the sky and has been Ulm's defining landmark since it was completed in 1890. Visitors who are not afraid of heights and narrow spaces can climb the 768 steps to the top of the spire. This energy-sapping endeavour is worth the effort, offering marvellous views across the region and to the Alps in the south.

Not quite so impressive was the elevation achieved by the Tailor of Ulm, Albrecht Berblinger, in 1811, when he attempted to fly with a self-built glider. He leapt from a riverside tower and promptly landed in the Danube. Nevertheless, his spirit of experimentation seems consistent with Ulm's claim that it is a city of science. Albert Einstein was born

in Ulm, and the University's new "research city" on the Eselsberg is home to numerous important research institutes.

Less difficult to understand than the theory of relativity, but possibly just as important, is bread. This basic staple of human nutrition is the subject of the Museum of Bread near the cathedral. Other important sites in the city include the town hall built in 1370 at the end of the fisherman's quarter. It features an astronomical clock and murals that show an Ulm barge on the river. In 1810, Napoleon incorporated the city of Ulm into the kingdom of Württemberg and the Danube became the border with Bavaria, allowing Neu Ulm to develop as a separate city.

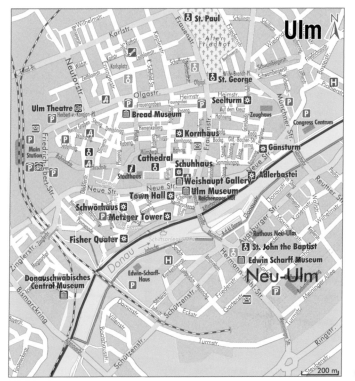

Ulm to Ingolstadt

The second stage of the tour covers the Danube valley between Ulm and Ingolstadt. A short distance past Ulm, riders cross into Bavaria, where the route remains for the rest of the distance to Passau. The landscape becomes flatter and you will pass inviting lakes and ride through wetland habitats, rich with plant and animal life, formed around the confluences of the Danube with numerous tributary rivers. The route

passes through or near historic old cities like Günzburg, Dillingen and Höchstädt, where aristocratic families and the church built impressive baroque and renaissance edifices. Parts of the route between Donauwörth and Neuburg are hillier as they cross the foothills of the Franconian Alb, which extends down to the Danube from the north. In Neuburg, the rider is welcomed by the impressive palace and romantic townscape before reaching the end of the section in Ingolstadt.

The route follows bicycle paths, quiet country lanes and unpaved paths and field and forest roads. There are only a few short stretches with heavier traffic, and almost no difficult climbs to be conquered.

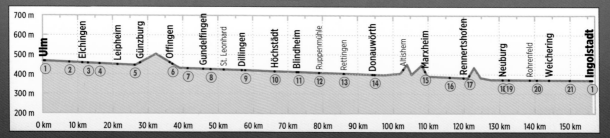

Ulm to Günzburg   28 km

When you cross the Danube in Ulm, you are also crossing the border between Baden-Württemberg and Bayern (Bavaria). The route will stay in the free state of Bavaria all the way to Passau, and you will become well accustomed to the beer, veal sausage (Weisswurst) and pretzel (Brezel) culture which has found such strong tradition here. Enjoy!

Neu-Ulm

Postal Code: 89231; Area code: 0731

- **Tourist-Information** Ulm/Neu-Ulm, 89073 Ulm, Münsterpl. 50, ✆ 1612830, www.neu-ulm.de
- **Edwin Scharff Museum**, Petruspl. 4, ✆ 9726180, Open: Tue, Wed 13-17, Thur-Sat 13-18, Sun 10-18. Permanent and changing exhibitions of the artist Edwin Scharff and his contemporaries. **Childrens Museum**.
- **Museum Walther Collection**, Reichenauerstr. 21, ✆ 1769143, Open: Thur-Sun by arrangement. International private collection of contemporarry photography and film from Africa and Asia.
- St. John the Baptist church (expressionist style)
- Glacis city park in the former fortress
- Donaubad Wonnemar, Wiblinger Str. 55, ✆ 985990.

- **Radweg**, Brückenstr. 1, Neu-Ulm, ✆ 9723890
- **Fahrrad Schmid**, Pfuhler Str. 34, Neu-Ulm/Offenhausen, ✆ 9716070
- **Tretbar Fahrradladen**, Spielbergstr. 12, Neu-Ulm/Pfuhl, ✆ 3782898

Continue along the river bank ～ **1** you pass below a road bridge, the Herdbrücke, and a little later another road bridge, the Gänstorbrücke, as you leave the centre of Ulm ～ as you follow the river you pass a large park, the **Friedrichsau** ～ after the park continue on the bicycle path next to **Thalfinger Uferstraße** ～ you pass a hydroelectric power station, the Donaukraftwerk Böfinger Halde.

> **TIP** Here the alternative route along the south bank rejoins the main route.

The roof landscape of Ulm

After the power station the bicycle path continues along the river ～ you come to follow the **Thalfinger Uferstraße** once more as you near Thalfingen, the path eventually switching to the left side of the road ～ continue past the railway station and the playing field before turning left into the **Donaustraße** by the little white church ～ **2** cross the railyway tracks into Thalfingen.

> **TIP** The scenic stretch along the river between Thalfingen and Leipheim is unfortunately closed to bicycles. The route therefore takes you away from the river for the next few kilometres.

Thalfingen

Postal Code: 89275; Area code: 0731

- **Town office**, Pfarrg. 2, ✆ 20660

Stay on **Donaustraße** ～ in the centre of town turn right at the post office onto **Elchinger Straße** ～ follow the wide bicycle path along the left side of **Elchinger Straße** out of the town.

Oberelchingen

Postal Code: 89275; Area code: 0731

- **Town office**, Thalfingen, ✆ 20660
- Abbey and pilgrimage church **St. Peter and Paul**

✻ **Martins gate** at the former abbey, Napoleon heights

☞ **Indoor pool**, Bildstöckle 1, ✆ 7261

⚠ Be careful at the busy intersection when entering Oberelchingen ～ continue along the bicycle path to Unterelchingen ～ the path ends just past the railway station.

Unterelchingen

200 m after the railway station turn right onto **Lange Straße** ～ ride parallel with the train tracks ～ at the next railway crossing turn right on **Hauptstraße** ～ keep left after crossing the tracks and continue on the bicycle path along the right side of **Weißinger Straße** ～ **3** proceed straight at the roundabout ～ and across the bridge over the A 7 freeway ～ continue parallel to the Weißinger Straße to Weißingen.

Weißingen

As you entre the village turn right into the first side street, **Ortsstraße** ～ in the centre of the village keep right and take the wide, straight gravel path into the forest, the "Weißinger Hölzle" ～ 1 km after the underpass under the A 8 freeway the route returns to the Danube ～ ride under the road bridge.

CENTRE ▌Here you can use the bridge to get you across the river into Leipheim.

Leipheim

Postal Code: 89340; Area code: 08221

ℹ **Tourist-Information Günzburg-Leipheim**, 89312 Günzburg, ✆ 200444, www.leipheim.de

🏛 **Local history and peasant uprising museum**, Stadtberg 1, ✆ 70721, Open: Sat, Sun 14-17.

🎇 **Historic Centre**: Parish church St. Veit (14th c.), city wall, fountain

🏰 **Leipheim Palace** (16th c.), private.

☞ **Gartenhallenbad**, Günzburger Str. 68, ✆ 71979

🔧 **Zweirad - Schlosserei Biedenbach**, Güssenstr. 25, ✆ 7555

A bridge guarded by a castle at the current site of Leipheim gave the town regional importance as early as 1063. In 1453 the city and its inhabitants were sold to Ulm for 23,200 gulden. On the second weekend of July, the city celebrates a children's festival, which was first held in 1818 to celebrate a good harvest after years of war, famine and hardship.

Another noteworthy site is a 600-year old linden, or lime, tree on the Lindenweg near the cemetery.

The route from Leipheim to Günzburg continues along the north bank of the Danube but away from the river ～ at first along the street **Weidlenweg** ～ turn right before the fields and the creek and follow the track through the riparian forests ～ you cross a bridge over a small tributary, the Nau, before coming to a T-intersection at the edge of the forest ～ turn right ～ cross to the other side of **Heidenheimer Straße** and turn right on the bicycle path along the left side of the street.

FORK ▌You now have the choice between two sign-posted routes. One route follows a flat gravel path along the Danube and bypasses both Günzburg and Offingen. The other passes through Günzburg and over the heights to Offingen, where the two routes reconnect. The Günzburg route is 2.5 km longer and has several mild climbs.

Günzburg to Gundelfingen   **18.5 km**

Along the north bank   *8.5 km*

5 Immediately after crossing a small bridge over the Nau, turn left into the park along the

18

N

Oberhaslach

Unterhaslach

Kesselbronn

Kugelberg
· 545

Böfingen

Böfinger Halde

Böfinger Waldstr.

Donau

Wasserkraftwerk Böfinger Halde

Pfuhler See

Röhrensee

Ulm Zoo

Friedrichsau

Pfuhl

Burlafingen

Walther Collection

Buchberg
· 495

Thalfingen

Böfinger Str.

Thalfinger See

Reitgries See

Donau

Karpfensee

Schwabsee

St. Peter and Paul

Elchingen

Dafernersee

Oberelchingen

Oberelchingen See

Vollmersee

Tannenteich

Weißinger Str.

Autobahnsee

Riedelsee

Eibisee

Leibi

Leibi

Roth

Nersingen

Roth

65

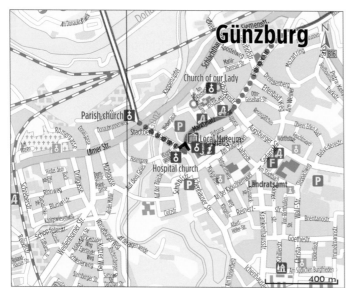

Günzburg

cross the road before continuing along the river.

After a long ride beside the river you pass a hydroelectric power station ~ after passing under a railway bridge you come to an intersection with a paved lane **6**. Here the route along the south bank comes from the right. Turn left to continue towards Gundelfingen. The route description continues by **6** on page 68.

On the south bank
via Günzburg **11 km**
If you wish to ride via Günzburg, **5** continue straight on the bicycle path along **Heidenheimer Straße** ~ you cross the Danube and the railway line ~ continue straight across the busy Ulmer Straße (B 10) ~ you cross the Günz along the street **Stadtberg** ~ after 200 m follow **Stadtberg** to the left ~ after a

short steep climb you ride through the Unteres Tor (lower gate) and straight along the **Marktplatz**.

Günzburg

Postal Code: 89312; Area code: 08221

🛈 **Tourist-Information Günzburg-Leipheim**, Schlosspl. 1, ☎ 200444, www.guenzburg.de

🏛 **Local museum** (1755-57), in the former Piarist college, Rathausg. 2, ☎ 38828, Open: Sat, Sun 14-17. Roman archaeology, city history, church art, folklore, mineralogy.

⛪ **Frauenkirche (Church of our Lady)** (1736-41), built by Dominik Zimmermann

🏰 **Renaissance palace** (1577-80) with **court church** and rococo chapel (18th c.), built by the Italian architect was Alberto Luchese for the archduke Ferdinand II for his son, who became the Margrave Karl.

🎡 **LEGOLAND**, Legoland Allee, ☎ 700700, Open: daily Apr.-Oct.

🎡 **Stadtturm/Unteres Tor (Lower gate)**, Open: The landmark is open Tue 10-14 Bavarian breakfast, 1st Sun/month coffee and cake. Great view over the city.

lane **In der Gmeind** ~ you pass the outdoor public pool ~ after the pool turn left over the bridge, crossing the Nau once again ~ keep right and follow the track down to the Danube ~ for the next

8 km you will ride on the gravel path directly beside the Danube ~ pass under the B 16 main road ~ by the bridge to Reisensburg, where you have the option of crossing to the south bank, you must

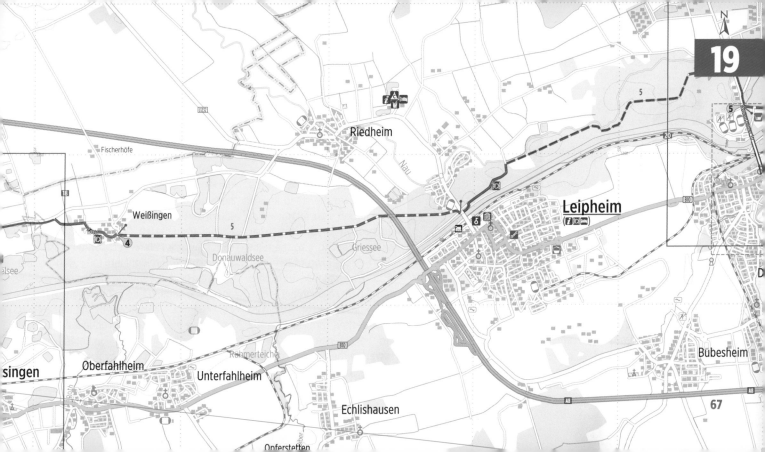

N

Riedheim

Fischerhöfe

18

Weißingen

4

5

Donauwaldsee

Griessee

Leipheim

6

5

20

B10

Oberfahlheim

Unterfahlheim

Rühmerteiche

B10

Echlishausen

Bubesheim

singen

A8

67

Onferstetten

- ✲ **Rathaus (Town hall)**, built between 1764-67 as a mint for the Austrian possessions, the Maria-Theresia Taler was made here until 1805.
- ▣ **Waldbad pool**, Heidenheimer Str. 2, ✆ 5422
- ▣ **Saiko's Velo**, Schlachthausstr. 37, ✆ 2049800
- ▣ **AFS GmbH**, Augsburger Str. 18a, ✆ 36400

Günzburg's best-known landmark is the Unterer Tor, or Lower Gate. Ride through it to arrive at the beautiful long Marktplatz and its many handsome old half-timbered houses with steep roofs typical for the region. The most important structure in the city is the rococo Frauenkirche, or Church of our Lady, built 1736-41 by Dominik Zimmermann.

At the far end of the Marktplatz proceed straight on **Dillinger Straße** ～ after 400 m turn right onto the bike path on the left side of **Reisensburger Straße** ～ the bike path on the side of the road ends at the cemetery at the edge of Reisensburg ～ proceed straight on **Günzburger Straße** into Reisensburg.

Stadtturm Günzburg

Reisensburg
Postal Code: 89312; Area code: 08821
- ▣ **Reisensburg Palace**, Bgm.-Joh.-Müller-Straße, ✆ 9070.

Continue to the T-intersection, where the connecting route between the north and south bank routes lies to the left. Turn right here onto the street **Mösle** ～ stay on Mösle as it curves to the left ～ ride up the steep incline ～ turn left on a gravel track that branches off where the street makes a sharp turn to the right ～ between fields turn left ～ at the next intersection turn right and follow the gravel path through the forest. The gravel path becomes a road of two paved tracks ～ at the intersection turn right on the paved street ～ in the distance you can now see the cooling towers of the Gundremmingen nuclear power plant ～ after about 2 km you reach Offingen.

Offingen
Postal Code: 89362; Area code: 08224
- ▣ **Council office**, Marktstr. 19, ✆ 96970
- ▣ **St. Georg parish church (1618)**, circular chapel

At the T-intersection turn left on **Hauptstraße** ～ continue past the church ～ turn right by the cemetery on **Donaustraße** ～ you pass below the railway line and continue to the intersection with the main road ～ turn left onto the bike path on the left side of the road ～ after crossing the Danube turn left on the paved side street ～ **6** after 150 m the two routes rejoin, the north bank route coming from the left. Continue along the paved street towards Peterswörth ～ after crossing the railway tracks turn right into the paved lane between the fields ～ continue straight until you pass an inn and bathing lake ～ **7** turn right before the playing fields ～ keep right by the tennis courts and follow the bicycle path unde the railway line and under the main road ～ in Peterswörth turn left where the path ends by the street.

Peterswörth
At the T-intersection turn left onto **Peterswörther Straße** ～ follow the street out of

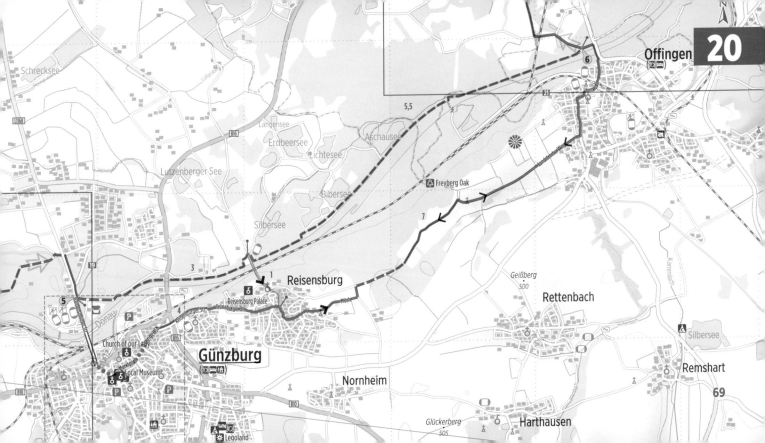

Schreksee

L1168

Langensee

Erdbeersee

Lichtesee

Lutzenberger See

Bibersee

Silbersee

Aschausee

Freyberg Oak

5,5

21

Offingen

20

6

1

Reisensburg

Reisensburg Palace
Grünbergenstr.

Mösle

7

Geißberg
500

Rettenbach

Silbersee

3

19

5

Donau

B16

Church of our Lady

Local Museum

Günzburg

Nornheim

Remshart

69

B10

Glückerberg
505

Harthausen

B10

Legoland

PetersWörth, where a bicycle path begins on the right hand side of the street ~ continue past **Stadionstraße**.

ALTERNATIVE A shorter alternative route to Echenbrunn begins here to the right on Stadionstraße.

Turn left at the next side street and ride through the railway underpass ~ follow the right bend on **Xaver-Schwarz-Straße** ~ and the left bend by the railway station onto **Bahnhofstraße**, which you follow into the centre of Gundelfingen.

Gundelfingen

Postal Code: 89423; Area code: 09073

- 🛈 **Culture office,** in the town hall, Prof.-Bamann-Str. 22, ✆ 999-118
- 🏛 **Automobile Museum Gundelfingen**, Bächinger Straße, ✆ 2575, Open: by arrangement.
- ✴ **Romantic city centre with** St. Martin church, Spital church, town hall, Schlachtegg, Torturm (gate tower).
- 🏊 **Bathing lakes** Gartnersee and Wünschsee

Schlachtegg Palace, Gundelfingen

🗒 **Hausmann,** Schulstr. 5-7, ✆ 7257

Gundelfingen is a romantic small city that is also sometimes called the city of gardners. With three arms of the river flowing through its centre, Gundelfingen lies between the meadows and flood plains of the Danube valley.

Gundelfingen apparently grew out of an outpost on the Roman road that passed here. The name seems to come from Gundolf, a local ruler in the third century after Christ.

Remnants of the old city walls and archaeological finds dating to the 6th and 7th centuries AD bear testament to the small city's long history.

Gundelfingen to Dillingen   11 km

After crossing three bridges, turn left onto **Prof.-Bamann-Straße** and ride through the town gate ~ turn right on **Hauptstraße** ~ turn right again on **Lauinger Straße** ~ follow the

bicycle path along the Lauinger Straße ~ after crossing the railway line you reach Echenbrunn.

Echenbrunn

8 turn right into **Leitenstraße** ~ you soon reach Faimingen ~ continue on **Magnus-Scheller-Straße**.

Faimingen

- ✴ **Apollo-Grannus-Temple**, free entry year round. Reconstruction of the largest Roman temple complex north of the alps.

After the Roman Temple make a left and right turn, then continue along **Kastellstraße** ~ at the next intersection turn left out to the main road, where you turn right onto the bicycle path along the **Gundelfinger Straße** through Lauingen.

Lauingen

Postal Code: 89415; Area code: 09072

- 🛈 **City office**, Herzog-Georg-Str. 17, ✆ 9980, www.lauingen.de
- 🏛 **Heimathaus der Stadt**, Herzog-Georg-Str. 57, ✆ 5491. Ehibits the old city signet and old Lauinger prints, a 16th c. St. Agnes statue and tools for farming and crafts.
- ✴ **St. Leonhard church**
- ✴ **Herzog Palace**, 15th c. core, with numerous additions and rennovations. Today it serves as a psychiatric home and therapeutic centre.

- ✱ **Battlement with gate** (Tränktor).
- ✱ **Marktplatz (market square)** with classicist **town hall** and **Schimmelturm (white horse tower)**.
- ✱ **Guided tours** by appointment, Herzog-Georg-Str. 17, ✆ 7030
- ✉ **Sports and recreation centre "Auwaldanlagen"**; swimming lake, Friedrich-Ebert-Str. 10, ✆ 2366

– Dillingen

- 🚲 **Bike & Tec**, Riedhauserstr. 3, ✆ 921250
- 🚲 **Siegbert Riesenegger**, Gundelfinger Str. 10, ✆ 3405
- 🚲 **Radhaus Lauingen**, Pfarrfeldstr. 1 ✆ 991808

Lauingen has one of the prettiest markets in Swabia, with its classicist town hall and monument for Albertus Magnus. Born in Lauingen in 1193, Magnus was a Dominican friar who is considered one of the great medieval philosophers of Germany. He advocated the peaceful coexistence of science and theology.

Faimingen, a suburb of Lauingen that also lies on the cycle route, contains interesting ruins of a Roman fortress, including the carefully restored ruins of the Apollo Grannus temple.

ALTERNATIVE Just after the hospital in Lauingen you have the opportunity to take a traffic free, alternative route on a unpaved route along the river. The main route on the other

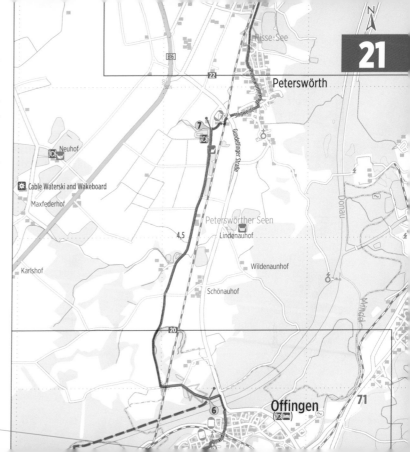

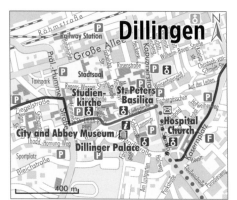

Dillingen

hand takes you through the historic centre of Lauingen.

For the quiet route to Dillingen turn right at the hospital onto the street **Oberer Wall** ~ which goes downhill and below the palace ~ stay left after the beer garden ~ and then left on the gravel **Segrepromenade** when you come to the Danube~ you pass under a road bridge~ continue on the Segrepromenade along the river bank ~ after 1.3 km ride past the wastewater treatment plant ~ turn left immediately after

passing under the bridge ~ after about 250 m turn right to rejoin the main route.

To follow the main route stay on the main street, now called the **Herzog-Georg-Straße**, past the church ~ continue straight through the historic centre, after which a biccycle path begins ~ turn right into the **Waihengeyerstra-ße** ~ left on **Herrgottsruhweg** ~ turn right into the street **In der Ludwigsau** ~ you pass a commercial building ~ follow the left bend to the main road, which you cross ~ continue straight ahead on the gravel road through a wooded area, the Waihengai ~ cross two bridges and entre Dillingen ~ then left up the hill to the first houses ~ follow **Mozartstraße** to the left ~ turn right on **Ziegelstraße** ~ at the T-intersection right, then left into the historic centre of the city.

Dillingen

Postal Code: 89407; Area code: 09071

🛈 **Tourist Information**, Königstr. 37/38, ✆ 54208, www.dillingen-donau.de

🏛 **Stadt und Hochstiftmuseum (city and abbey museum)**, Am Hafenmarkt 11, ✆ 4400, Open: Wed 14-17, every 1st and 3rd Sun 14-17.

Prehistory, Roman times, crafts, university and military exhibits, smithy.

🏰 **Dillinger Palace** (former prince-bishop's residence)

⛪ **Studienkirche (1616-1617)** and former university with "**Golden hall**", Open: Apr.-Oct., Sat, Sun 10-17.

⛪ **St. Peter's Basilica**

✹ **Historic centre**.

✹ **Guided tours**: Apr.-Oct., Sun 2 pm, public tour starting at the town hall (Rathaus), group tours by appointment at the tourism office.

🚲 Lockable **bicycle parking boxes**, Carpark Hofbrauhaus/Stadtmitte and at the train station (bring a lock!)

🛁 **Indoor pool**, Ziegelstr. 10, ✆ 703701

🏊 **Eichwaldbad**, Heated outdoor pool, Oblatenweg 10, ✆ 71582

🔧 **Top-Bike-Brachem**, Am Stadtberg 21, ✆ 6222

Dillingen was shaped by the presence of senior clerics and church intellectuals. It was the seat of power for the prince-bishops of Augsburg who ruled a large territory. The establishment of a university by Jesuits added to the city's influence. It is also one of the few German cities that did not suffer damage during World War Two. It was in Dillingen that the clerical scholar Sebastian Kneipp invented the cold-water therapy that bears his name. He claimed that

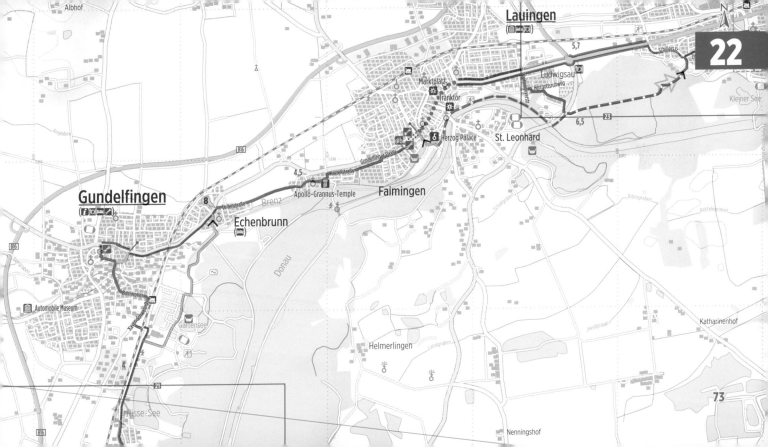

Albhof

Lauingen

22

5,7

Ludwigsau
Herrgottsruhweg

Kleiner See

Marktplatz

Franktor

6,5 23

Herzog Palace

St. Leonhard

B16

4,5

Kastellstraße

Gundelfinger Straße

Faimingen

Apollo-Grannus-Temple

Gundelfingen

8

Leitenstraße

Echenbrunn

Brenz

Donau

Biblisgraben

Rottelegraben

Katharinenhof

Automobile Museum

Bahnhofstraße

Gartensee

Helmerlingen

Landgraben

Schafgraben

Heidgraben

B16

21

Flisse-See

Nenningshof

regular dips in the cold Danube helped cure a lung ailment.

Dillingen to Höchstädt   6.5 km

Ride through the historic centre ~ after the city gate take the main street, **Am Stadtberg,** to the right ~ continue to the roundabout **9**.

FORK At the roundabout you once again have the choice of two routes. You can either take the direct route to Steinheim along the main road or take the unpaved, but considerably more attractive, route along the Danube.

Along the Danube to Steinheim   7 km

9 Go straight through the roundabout ~ follow the **Donaustraße** down to the Danube ~ turn left directly before the bridge onto the street **Nachtweide** ~ after 150 m turn right down to the river bank ~ then left and onto the gravel path ~ through the pretty flood plains directly next to the river ~ keep left past numerous ponds towards Steinheim.

Steinheim

Turn right at the T-intersection ~ after the playing fields keep left and cross the bridge ~ continue straight ahead into **Jägerstraße** ~ turn right into **Römerstraße** ~ then left into **Makromannenstraße** ~ at the main road (B 16) you turn right, where you rejoin the other route from Dillingen, which comes from the left.

Direct Route to Steinheim   4.5 km

9 At the roundabout turn left (3rd exit) onto the street **Kasernplatz** ~ turn right into the street **Am Galgenberg** ~ continue to the commercial area, where you turn left on **Gutenbergstraße** ~ at the T-intersection turn right on **Rudolf-Diesel-Straße** ~ at the end of the street change to the bicycle path along the main road (B 16) to Steinheim.

Steinheim

🚲 **Radler Oase** (cyclists rest) with water, picnic tables, shelter, air pump

Continue along the main road through the town ~ a bicycle path begins again on the right side of the road as you leave Steinheim, where you

Marktplatz in Höchstädt

are rejoined by the route along the Danube from Dillingen ~ continue along the main road to the **Marktplatz** (market square) in Höchstädt.

Höchstädt a. d. Donau

Postal Code: 89420; Area code: 09074

🛈 Tourism office, Herzog-Philipp-Ludwig-Str. 10, ☎ 4412, www.hoechstaedt.de

🏛 Local Museum (Heimatmuseum), Marktpl. 7, ☎ 4412, Open: Apr.-Sept., Sun 14-16, Oct.-Mar., by arrangement. Folklore, religious art, Easter egg collection, tin-figure diorama of the battle of Höchstädt-Blenheim.

🏛 Museum of German faience, in Schloss Höchstädt, Herzogin-Anna-Str. 52, ☎ 9585-700, Open: Apr.-Sept., Tue-Sun 9-18. Exhibits cover the battle of 1704, Swabian history and ceramics of the 17th and 18th c.

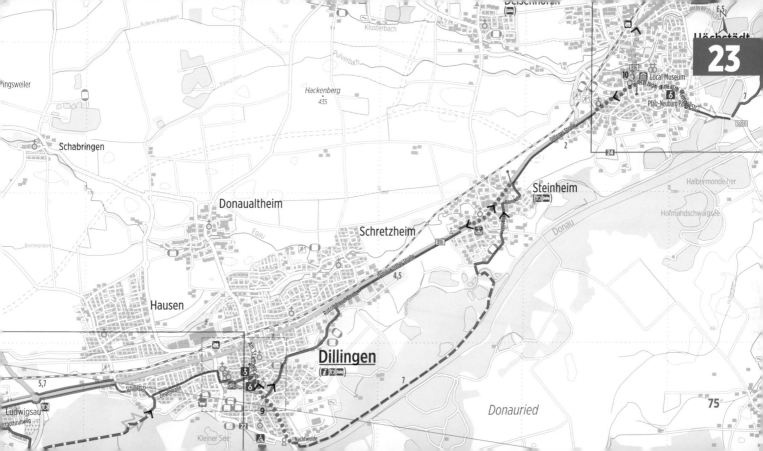

Deisenhofen

Klosterbach

Pulverbach

Außerer Riedgraben

ingsweiler

Hackenberg
· 435

Schabringen

Local Museum

Herzog-

Pfalz-Neuburg Palace

Dillinger Straße

2

Halbermondeiher

Steinheim

Donaualtheim

Römersee

Schretzheim

Hofmahdschwaigsee

Egau

B16

Donau

Breitlegraben

4,5

Donauwörther Straße

Hausen

Rudolf-Diesel-Straße

Dillingen

7

Am Stadtberg

5

6

5,7

Ludwigsau

Schillerstr.

Ziegelstraße

9

Donauried

rgottsruhweg

Kleiner See

22

Nachtweide

75

Höchstädt Palace

- 🖼 **Mariä Himmelfahrt** parish church (1442), late gothic church, choir stalls, baptismal font, sacramental booth
- 🏛 **Schloss Höchstädt**, Herzogin-Anna-Str. 52, ✆ 9585-700. Palace of the Palsgraves of Pfalz-Neuburg, four-wing Renaissance structure, palace chapel with noteworthy ceiling paintings, cultural events, café. Also houses the Museum of German faience.
- ✳ **Memorial** "Tracing the tracks of 1704", 23 km bicycle route with information about the landscape and tactics of the battle, written description also available at ✆ 4412
- ✳ **City tours**, May-Oct., every 3rd Sun/month, 13:30, staring from the palace.

The picturesque old city of Höchstädt is famous for the decisive battle fought here during the War of the Spanish Succession. Allied armies

led by Prince Eugene of Savoy and the Duke of Marlborough defeated a French-Bavarian army that was seeking to capture Vienna and force an end to the war. English speaking peoples call this the Battle of Blenheim.

Höchstädt to Donauwörth   29 km

ALTERNATIVE The shorter alternative route along the road to Sonderheim begins at the Marktplatz in Höchstädt.

TIP Make sure you have enough food and beverages before leaving Höchstädt, as there are few shopping opportunities until Donauwörth.

10 The main route departs the **Marktplatz** in Höchstädt on **Herzogin Anna Straße** ~ ride past the palace ~ after a curve to the left continue down **Wertinger Straße**, a bicycle path begins as you leave Höchstädt ~ after 700 m follow the bike route sign towards Sonderheim to the left ~ the paved lane takes you between fields and ponds to Sonderheim.

Sonderheim

In Sonderheim turn right at the T-intersection ~ after leaving the village, keep left ~ turn right

and follow the bicycle path beside the road to Blindheim ~ the path ends as you reach the first houses.

Blindheim

- ✳ noteworthy **Heimathaus** with an ornamented column from 1704
- ✳ **Natural Kneipp baths** (near the turn-off to Gremheim on the Danube bicycle route)

Blindheim saw much of the action in what was the costliest battle in the War of the Spanish Succession. The "Book of History" monument on the town square stands as a reminder and call for peace.

Follow the main street, at first called **Höchstädter Straße**, then **Bahnhofstraße**, through Blindheim ~ **11** turn right on **Mühlstraße** ~ a bicycle path begins on the left side after 300 m ~ keep left on the **Hauptstraße** as you reach Gremheim.

Gremheim

EXCURSION To reach the Kalteneck water palace in Schwenningen, turn left into the **Jurastraße**.

Schwenningen

Postal code: 89443; Area code: 09070

- 🏛 **Schloss Kalteneck**, Kirchstr. 26b, ✆ 909940. The oldest surviving parts of the orignal water castle date from before 1140, possibly

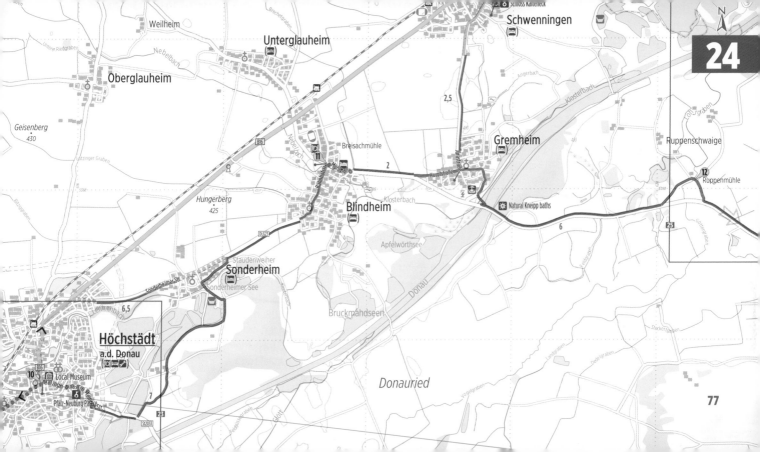

Weilheim

Unterglauheim

Oberglauheim

Geisenberg
430

Schloss Kalteneck

Schwenningen

2,5

Gremheim

Ruppenschwaige

12
Ruppenmühle

816

Hungerberg
· 425

11

Breisachmühle

2

Hauptstraße

Natural Kneipp baths

25

6

Blindheim

Klosterbach

Apfelwörthsee

Donau

DLG53

Staudenweiher

Sonderheim

Sonderheimer See

6,5

Bruckmähdseen

Höchstädt
a.d. Donau

10

Local Museum

816

7

Pfalz-Neuburg Palace

23

SP203

Donauried

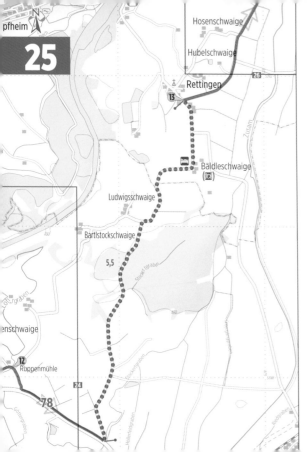

Hosenschwaige

Hubelschwaige

Rettingen

26

13

Zusum

Bäldleschwaige

Ludwigsschwaige

Bärtlstockschwaige

5,5

Stock grāben

nschwaige

12
Ruppenmühle

24

78

Schloss Kalteneck, Schwenningen

as early as 950. The castle was rebuilt as a water palace in Renaissance style around 1570.

Follow the **Hauptstraße** through Gremheim ~ after two right bends you leave the village ~ turn left on the paved bicycle path before reaching the main road ~ follow the path up to and over the bridge across the danube ~ continue on the bicycle path along the main road until it comes to an end ~ turn left onto a small road ~ **12** keep right as you pass the **Ruppenmühle** ~ you return to the main road ~ turn left and follow the bicycle path along the main road once again ~ after 1.3 km you

reach a side road, where you turn left towards Donauwörth ~ follow this road for the next 10 km between fields to Rettingen.

Rettingen

13 At the first intersection in Rettingen turn right towards Zusum.

Zusum

One kilometer after Zusum turn left on a gravel path, which takes you out to a barrage on the Danube ~ ride straight across the barrage ~ turn right on the paved lane **Am Kesseldamm** ~ as you pass under a road bridge the street becomes the **Industriestraße** ~ you pass the Eurocopter factory complex ~ continue along **Gartenstraße** after passing under the railway bridge.

Turn right at the main road ~ after a few meters turn left on **Hindenburgstraße** and cross the Wörnitz River onto **Ried Island** ~ continue straight ahead and cross the old bridge through the city gate into the historic centre of Donauwörth ~ along **Spitalstraße** and straight into **Rathausgasse** ~ straight past the Tourist Information and through a small gate in the city wall ~ after crossing the stream, turn right on the promenade through the park.

Donauwörth

Postal Code: 86609; Area code: 0906

🄸 **City Tourist Information**, Rathausg. 1, ✆ 789151, www.donauwoerth.de

🏛 **Archaeological Museum** in the Tanzhaus, Reichsstr. 34, Open: all year Sat, Sun/Hol 14-17.

🏛 **Local Museum** on the Ried Island, Museumspl. 2, Open: May-Oct., Tue-Sun 14-17, Nov.-Apr. Wed, Sat, Sun/Hol 14-17.

Donauwörth

🏛 **City History House**, Rieder Tor, Open: by appt., ✆798170, or 798151

🏛 **Käthe-Kruse Doll Museum**, Pflegstr. 21a, Open: May-Sept., Tue-Sun 11-18, Oct.-Apr., Thur-Sun 14-17.

🏛 **Werner Egk house**, Pflegstr. 21a, Open: May-Sept., Tue-Sun 11-18, Oct.-Apr., Thur-Sun 14-17. Art and culture for music lovers.

🄷 **Church of Our Lady Cathedral (Münster)**, 15th c. gothic hall-church has one of Swabia's biggest church bells, the 6.5 ton "Pummerin"

🄷 **Heilig Kreuz Abbey**, 11th c. pilgrim church with Baroque decor from the "Wessobrunn School", artistically significant interior.

✺ **Deutschordenshaus (House of the Knights of the Teutonic Order)**, 18th c., one of the oldest branches of the order founded in 1197.

✺ **Reichsstraße**. One of the most beautiful streets in southern Germany, with Rathaus, Tanzhaus, gothic minster, Fuggerhaus and Reichsstadt fountain.

✺ **Café Engel**, former seat of the Donauwörth master singers school, oldest documented house in the city.

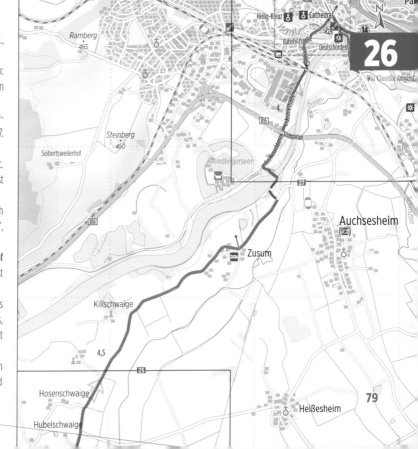

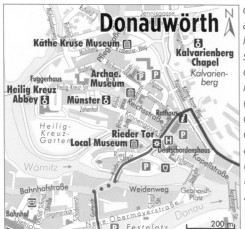

Donauwörth N

- Käthe Kruse Museum
- Fuggerhaus
- Heilig Kreuz Abbey
- Münster
- Archae. Museum
- Kalvarienberg Chapel
- Kalvarienberg
- Rathaus
- Heilig-Kreuz-Garten
- Rieder Tor
- Local Museum
- Deutschordenshaus

Wörnitz

Bahnhofstraße
Bahnhof
Weidenweg
Gebhardt Platz
Donau
Festplatz

200 m

✉ **Outdoor pool on the** Schellenberg, Sternschanzenstr. 3, ✆ 789540

🚲 **Zwei-Rad Uhl**, Dillinger Str. 57, ✆ 9816060

🚲 **Top Bike Brachem**, Kapellstr. 25, ✆ 8077

Today it is difficult to imagine that a single bridge can mean prosperity and riches to a city. But long ago, when building a longer bridge was a difficult and expensive proposition, this was often the case, as in Donauwörth. This was where the important trading route between Nuremberg and Augsburg crossed the Danube. The bridge was destroyed almost 30 times, and rebuilt just as often. The handsome city houses and the graceful Reichstraße underscore the city's historical significance, as do the numerous valuable artworks in the city's churches. One example is the Pietá (1508), an early baroque image, a stone statue of Maria, and the gothic sacramental booth. One end of the Reichstraße is defined by the Rathaus and the so-called Fuggerhaus, built by Anton Fugger between 1537-39 after being awarded the protectorate of the town.

A barracks for soldiers built near the city wall in 1715 is open to the public today. Other surviving remnants of the city wall include the Riedertor, the last of four main entrance gates to the city, and the Färbertor, one of the 38 towers that once guarded the wall.

Among the stories associated with the Holy Cross Abbey is one related to the relic of the holy cross which Graf Mangold I. brought from Byzantium. He had gone to Byzantium for a bride for the Emperor's son, a mission he was unable to fulfil.

Donauwörth to Bertoldsheim   21.7 km

Take the Promenade through the park ～ **14** at the end of the park turn left on the busy **Zirgesheimer Straße** ～ you pass under the large road bridge as you leave Donauwörth ～ a bicycle path along the right side of the road takes you to Zirgesheim.

Zirgesheim

As you pass Zirgesheim the bicycle path switches to the left side of the road ～ just before **Altisheim** the path ends ～ follow **Gartenstraße** to the left into the village ～ keep right back down to the main road, where you turn left and continue to Leitheim ～ a bicycle path begins on the right hand side.

Donauwörth

Leitheim

⛪ **Leitheim Palace**, Schloßstr. 1, ☎ 09097/1016.
  Concerts during summer months.

Turn left just after the palace ~ take the first street, **An der Leiten**, to the right ~ follow this paved field road back along the main road to Graisbach.

Graisbach

🏛 **Graisbach Ruin**

Turn left into the first side street ~ take the next street to the right and ride back to the main road ~ follow the bicycle path along the left side of the road to Lechsend.

Lechsend

Follow the main road through the village, then onto the bicycle path along the right side of the main road to Marxheim while enjoying the wonderful view over the Danube valley.

Marxheim

15 Turn right towards Bruck just after the church.

Bruck

Turn left as you reach Bruck ~ pass the playing field and keep left after the tennis courts ~ follow the unpaved path beside the dike along the Danube until you reach a recreational area with a small jetty ~ keep left here and follow the paved lane into Bertoldsheim ~ straight ahead onto **Seestraße**.

Bertoldsheim

Postal Code: 86643; Area code: 08434

ℹ **Visitors information Neuburg**, Neuburg an der Donau, ☎ 08431/55-240 or 241, www.neuburg-donau.de

⛪ **Baroque palace** (1718-30), built by the Eichstätt architect Gabriel de Gabrieli for the imperial General Freiherr Fortunat von Isselbach

⛪ **St. Michael parish church** (early 14th c.), gothic frescoes from 1340.

❀ **Sailing Lake**

Bertoldsheim to Neuburg   15 km

At the T-intersection turn left onto **Burgheimer Straße** ~ **16** take the second street to the right, **Bräuhausstraße** ~ keep right onto **Marxheimer Straße** and ride straight past the church and the inn ~ turn left in front of the palace ~ keep right into the lane **An der Allee** ~ cross the main road and continue on the paved field road ~ follow this road as it winds its way between the fields all the way to Hatzenhofen.

Hatzenhofen

Turn right after crossing the small bridge into the village ~ continue straight onto the **Hatzenhofener Straße** towards Stepperg.

Stepperg

⛪ **Palace**, main building erected by the Welser in the 16th century. Two wings added in 1805.

⛪ **St. Anton and St. Anna pilgrimage church** with tomb (1676), preserved frescoes and ceiling paintings. Built by Freiherr Dom. von Servi.

The small pilgrimage church stands idyllically placed on the Antoniberg bluff directly above the Danube.

Keep right at the fork into **Usselstraße** ~ follow the left curve of the street ~ then right on **Rennertshofener Straße** which soon becomes **Antonibergstraße** ~ **17** follow this street to the left and continue straight down the tree-lined avenue ~ an unpaved track takes you through a wooded area ~ keep right in the fields before reaching the main road ~ ride stright into Riedensheim.

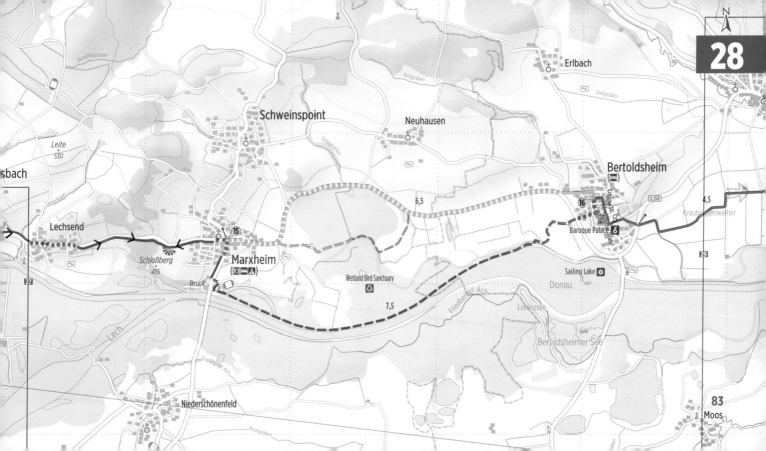

28

Erlbach

Schweinspoint

Neuhausen

Bertoldsheim

Leite
530

...sbach

Lechsend

16

6,5

4,5

Schloßberg
435

15

Baroque Palace

Marxheim

Bruck

Wetland Bird Sanctuary

Sailing Lake

7,5

Donau

Lorenzsee

27

Lech

Bertildsheimer See

Krautgräbenweiher

29

Niederschönenfeld

Moos

Riedensheim

Keep right at the T-intersection ~ follow the street to the right back out of the village ~ after the houses take the first turn left and ride along the forest edge down to the river ~ follow the unpaved track along the river, where you pass through the Finkenstein nature reserve ~ continue between fields ~ keep left on the road towards **Bittenbrunn** ~ ride

straight up to the main road, where you turn right towards Neuburg ~ continue along the bicycle path to the large intersection ~ turn right and cross the Danube into the historic centre of Neuburg.

Neuburg an der Donau

Postal Code: 86633; Area code: 08431

ℹ Tourist Information, Ottheinrich Pl. A 118, ✆ 55-240 or -241, www.neuburg-donau.de

🏛 Palace museum, Residenzstr. A 2, ✆ 6443-0, Open: Oct.-Mar., Tue-Sun 10-16, Apr.-Sept., Tue-Sun 9-18. Part of the Bavarian state collection of paintings, Flemish baroque paintings, baroque tombs in the garden, prehistory museum, religious tradition.

🏛 Palace museum and **State gallery of Flemish Baroque Paintings**, Residenzschloss, Residenzstr. 2, ✆ 64430, Open: Apr.-Sept., Tue-Sun 9-18, Oct.-Mar., Tue-Sun 10-16.

🏛 City museum, Weveldhaus, Amalienstr. 19, Open: Mar.-Dec., Tue-Sun 10-18.

🛐 Seminary church and school, former Ursuline cloister with cloister church from 1700, today Catholic academy.

🛐 Residence palace, early renaissance complex from the 16th c. with palace church (oldest protestant church in Bavaria), Sgraffiti in the courtyard plus **Museum** and **State Gallery** for Flemish baroque paintings.

🛐 Former Mint, castle from 1200 built on a prehistoric Celtic defensive position. Served as a mint in the 16th c. Restored in 1989.

✱ Provincial library, early Rococo structure from the 18th c. designed by F. M. v. Loew, baroque chamber in the upper floor. Library since 1803. Guided tours: May-Oct, Wed 14:30.

✱ Rathaus (Town Hall), renaissance town hall from the early 16th c., ground floor contains city art gallery.

✱ Weveldhaus, Adelspalais with renaissance and baroque stylistic elements, stuccoed chambers. Contains the city museum.

✱ baroque court pharmacy from the 18th c. Jazz club in the vaulted cellar spaces.

🏊 Parkbad (indoor water park),Ludwig-Thoma-Pl. 1, ✆ 61980

🏊 Outdoor pool Brandlbad, Am Unteren Brandl, ✆ 509146

🚲 Fahrrad Appel, Ingolstädter Str. 20, ✆ 9076819

🚲 Kneißl, Sternstr. 180, ✆ 42428

🚲 Zweirad Behr, Münchener Str. 162, ✆ 44889

Neuburg Palace from the Danube

Galgenberg
451

Gietlhausen

Rennertshofen

Treidelheim

Mühlberg
470

Dittenfeld

Platte
485

Laisacker

Hatzenhofen

Riedensheim

Stepperg

3

Bittenbrunn

Hatzenhofener Steige

Ussel

Antonibergstraße

17 6

Finkenstein Nature Reserve

7

30

Rathaus

St. Anton and St. Anna Pilgrimage Church

18

Former Mint

Donau

Mooser Schütt

Buchberg
445

Flachsberg
465

Kaiserburg

Höfelhof

B16

Kreut

Kramelsberg
450

Kreutzberg
430

Unterhausen

Oberhausen

Schwarzgraben

28

Schönbühl
440

Sehensand

B16

B16

Bike Markt, Münchener Str. 169, ✆ 42573

Key avail. against depostit from the Tourist-Information.

From 742 to 801 Neuburg was a bishopric seat. It first became part of Bavaria in 1247, and then became the residential seat of the principality of Palatinate-Neuburg in 1505. In 1777 it returned to Bavaria. The most distinctive structure in the small city is the large Neuburg palace, which some call the most beautiful renaissance palace on the Danube. It has an enchanting interior courtyard with 2-storey balconies. The chapel was built on orders of Duke Ottheinrich between 1530 and 1550 and is sometimes called the Bavarian Sistine chapel for its frescoes by H. Bocksberger.

Neuburg to Ingolstadt   22.1 km

18 After crossing the bridge, turn right after the first building ⌁ turn right again in front of the gate and ride under the bridge ⌁ continue into the street **Oskar Wittmann Straße** and ride along the bicycle path ⌁ follow the right bend of the street away from the river ⌁ continue straight beside **Grünauer Straße**.

Karlsplatz in Neuburg an der Donau

For those who would rather ride along the river, we recommend taking the alternative route.

Turn left into the wood before the industrial area begins ⌁ follow the dike along the river to the barrage across the Danube ⌁ cross the river and turn right ⌁ continue along the other side of the river to Ingolstadt.

19 Continue straight on the bicycle path past the industrial area ⌁ ride straight ahead through the roundabout towards the Grünau Palace. *The Au (wetland) begins east of this roundabout. The charming palace that graces the front cover of this book is the royal hunting lodge Grünau*

and is located less than a kilometer past the main road.

Grünau

Grünau hunting palace with **Wetland centre Neuburg/Donau**, Open: Wetland Informationcentre Apr.-Oct., Wed-Fri 9-12 & 13-18, Sat, Sun/Hol 10-18, Nov.-Mar., Sun 10-17.

In addition to the "Neue Burg" on the banks of the Danube in Neuburg, Graf Ottheinrich also built Grünau as a hunting palace and summer residence for his wife Suzanna. The renaissance structure, situated in an idyllic woods near the river, also houses a wetland information centre with exhibits detailing wetland ecology.

On the other side of the palace turn right and ride to **Rohrenfeld** ⌁ keep left at the fork and ride out of the village ⌁ in the right bend turn left into the gravel lane, which you follow between fields ⌁ **20** at the edge of the forest turn right and continue to Weichering.

Weichering

Turn left after crossing the railway tracks and ride into the village ⌁ take the next turn left across a small bridge, then immediately right ⌁ keep left at the intersection ⌁ ride straight

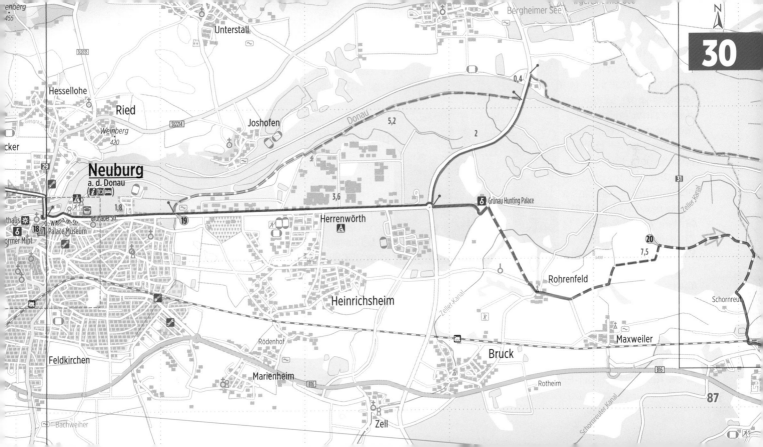

and follow the **Bahnhofstra-ße** out of the village ~ you pass under the railway line and proceed straight ~ follow the street to the left over a small bridge ~ immediately turn right onto a paved lane ~ continue straight onto the unpaved path through the wooded floodplain until you pass a house next to the track **21**.

ALTERNATIVE Here you have access to an unpaved path that follows the river into the city. You rejoin the main route by the park after the barrage.

Continue straight on the bicycle path along the dike into Ingolstadt ~ you ride past the Glacisbrücke and then the Konrad-Adenauer-Brücke.

CENTRE The historic centre of Ingolstadt on the other bank of the river can be easily reached across the Konrad-Adenauer-Brücke.

Kreuztor in Ingolstadt

Ingolstadt

Postal Code: 85049; Area code: 0841

🛈 Tourist Information, Altes Rathaus, Rathauspl. 2, ✆ 3053030, www.ingolstadt-tourismus.de

🏛 **Bavarian army museum,** in the Neues Schloss, Paradepl. 4, ✆ 93770, Open: Tue-Fri 9-17:30, Sat, Sun 10-17:30.

🏛 **History of Medicine Museum,** in the Alte Anatomie, Anatomiestr. 18-20, ✆ 3052860, Open: Tue-Sun 10-17.

🏛 **Museum of Concrete Art**, Tränktor Str. 6-8, ✆ 3051871, Open: Tue-Sun 10-17.

🏛 **Audi museum mobile,** in the Audi Forum, Ettinger Str., ✆ 8937575 or ✆ 0800/2834444, Open: Mon-Sun 9-18.

🏛 **City Museum and Toy Museum,** in the Kavalier Hepp, Auf der Schanz 45, ✆ 3051885, Open: Tue-Fri 9-17, Sat, Sun 10-17.

🏛 **Niemes-Prachatitz Museum**, Pedellhaus, Hohe-Schul-Str. 2, ✆ 1285357. Open: Every 2nd Sun/month, 14-16, free entry. Local history collections from the towns of Niemes and Prachatitz in Bohemia, which were transferred to Ingolstadt after WWII.

🔯 **St. Moritz church,** Ingolstadt's oldest church (built 1234)

🔯 **Asam church of Maria de Victoria** (1732-36), Neubaustr. 1½, ✆ 17518, Open: Mar.-Oct., Tue-Sun 9-12 & 13-17, May-Sept., Mon-Sun 9-12 & 13-17, Nov.-Feb., Tue-Sun 13-16.

🔯 **Cathedral,** late gothic hall church (1425)

🔯 **Neues Schloss (New Palace).** One of the most important secular buildings in Bavaria, it was built in the 15th c for Ludwig VII. von Bayern-Ingolstadt. Now houses the Bavarian Army Museum.

✳ **Kreuztor** (1385) medieval city gate.

🔳 **Little Zoo Wasserstern**, Gerolfinger Str./ Aloisiweg 19, ✆ 0176/43002631, Open:Apr.-Oct., Mon-Fri 15-18, Sat 13-18, Sun/Hol 9:30-18.

🔲 **Radhaus,** Bei der Arena 7, ✆ 885772-0

🔲 **Radhaus,** Kreuztor 2, ✆ 32211

Theresienstraße, Ingolstadt

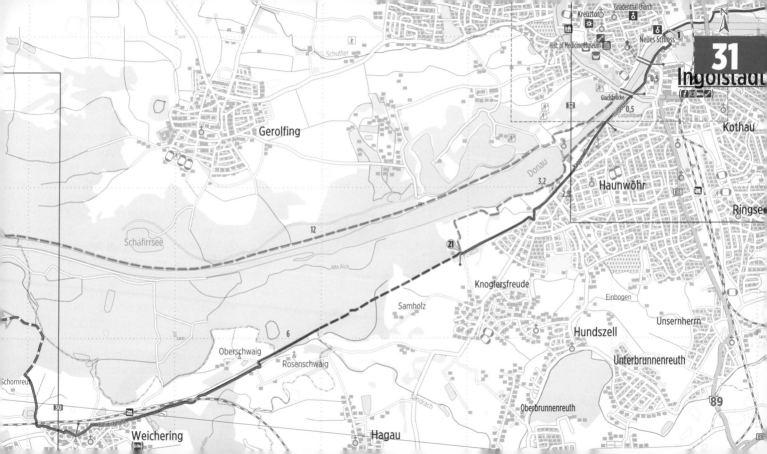

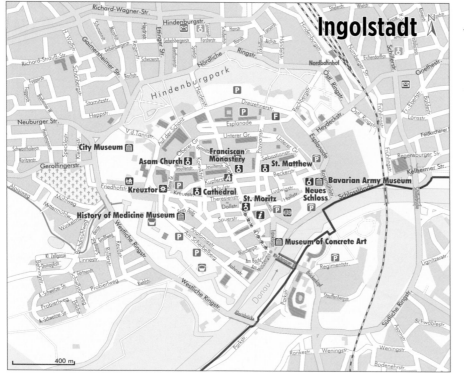

Ingolstadt

Ingolstadt (pop. 120,000) offers something for just about every visitor, but especially for anyone interested in art and history.

The earliest known record of the city documents that it already existed in 806. Ingolstadt gained city status in 1250. The most significant structures in the city include the large late gothic cathedral, the Neues Schloss, and the rococo Maria de Victoria church, which contains the so-called Lepanto monstrace. Created by the Augsburg goldsmith Johann Zeckel over the course of 30 years, it depicts the victory over the Turkish fleet at Lepanto in 1571.

Fans of horror stories can pursue the legend of Frankenstein's monster. Mary Shelley set her novel "Frankenstein, or, The Modern Prometheus" in Ingolstadt.

For hot and tired cyclists looking for refreshment, what could be more welcome than a stein of Bavarian beer? It was in Ingolstadt that the famous Bavarian "Reinheitsgebot" or "purity law" was first drafted in 1516 to assure the quality of beer. The city once boasted 25 breweries. Today only four remain, but the product they brew is considered some of the best beer in the world.v

Ingolstadt to Regensburg

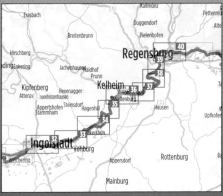

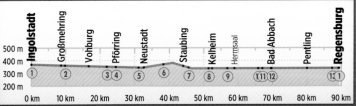

The third stage of your ride begins in Ingolstadt. The first kilometers follow the still-placid Danube to the small city of Vohburg with its city walls and gates that have witnessed some 1200 years of history. The Danube then enters a more dramatic stretch, as it enters the narrow gorge where the river's waters have forced their way through the Franconian Jura mountains between Weltenburg and Kelheim. We recommend taking a boat for this short stretch, which is much more relaxing and enjoyable than the route over the hills, and offers spectacular views of the breathtaking scenery. After Kelheim the river makes another couple of bends before reaching its northern most point in Regensburg. This spectacular city offers everything a tourists heart desires.

Most of this stage follows quiet country lanes, car-free bicycle paths and paths along the river. There are, however, several short stretches with heavier traffic and a few brief climbs.

Ingolstadt to Vohburg   17 km

From the south end of the Konrad-Adenauer-Brücke continue on the bicycle path along the river bank ～ ride up onto the bicycle and pedestrian bridge and cross to the north bank of the Danube ～ **1** turn right and follow the bicycle path parallel to the main road ～ you pass under a railway bridge and a road bridge ～ after the bend to the left, turn right and follow the path along the top of the dike out of Ingolstadt.

ALTERNATIVE Before the route entres Kleinmehring it passes over a very narrow bridge, which is difficult to negotiate when towing a trailer. Those who wish can therefore continue straight ahead along the dike to Großmehring or even as far as the barrage at Vohburg, which bypasses the busy bridge by Großmehring!

Turn left after the power station ～ by the main road turn left ～ follow the trail, keeping right ～ turn right as you reach a street, then immediately left into the narrow path ～ turn right and pass under the main road ～ continue

along **Nibelungenstraße** ～ keep right into **Uferstraße** ～ at the end of the street you reach the **Donaustraße**, the centre of Großmehring lies to the left.

Großmehring
Postal Code: 85098; Area code: 08407

🛈 **Rathaus**, Marienpl. 7, ☎ 9294-0
✉ **Hallermeier**, Marienpl. 3, ☎ 9153

Turn right and immediately right again into a small street over a bridge.

ALTERNATIVE To stay on the north bank, turn left after the small bridge, then right after the underpass and through another underpass to the track along the river.

Otherwise continue straight ahead and make your way up to the bridge and cross the Danube ～ on the south bank of the river turn right onto the unpaved road along the river ～ ride under the main road and continue on the small road next to the river ～ keep right by the barrage, where the route along the north bank rejoins the main route from the left ～ after crossing a small bridge take the next turn to the left onto the path along

Vohburg

the top of the dike ～ follow the dike into Vohburg.

ALTERNATIVE A short detour around the Burgberg and through the historic centre of Vohburg is well worth while.

After passing the first houses turn off the dike to the street **Auertorstraße**, which takes you through a town gate ～ turn right after the gate and follow the **Burgstraße** around the castle hill ～ by the bridge turn left through another town gate and follow the **Donaustraße** through the historic centre to the bridge over the Danube.

32

Oberhaunstadt

Unterhaunstadt

Raffinerie

Katharinenberg

Großer Weinberg
460

Kleiner Weinberg
· 395

Steinberg
· 395

Laimberg
460

Ingolstadt

Mailing

B16a

Großmehring

Kleinmehring

Feldkirchen

6,5

Mailinger See

Weinzierlweiher

Donau

3,4

Ilterstraße

Neues Schloss

0,5

Gnadenthal Church

?

2

Kothau

Auwaldsee

Paar

2

B13

aunwöhr

Ringsee

Vohburg

Postal Code: 85088; Area code: 08457

- ℹ️ **City office**, Ulrich-Steinberger-Pl. 12/13, ✆ 92920
- ✴️ **Burgberg** with old castle and **St. Peter parish church**, dates to 1500.
- 🛏️ **Outdoor heated pool**, Irsching near Vohburg, Paarstr. 20, ✆ 7626, Open: Sat, Sun/Hol 10-19, May, Sept, Tue-Fri 13-20, Jun.-Aug., Tue-Fri 10-20.
- ✴️ **Maschinen-Miet-Service**, Paarstr. 27a, Irsching, ✆ 1587

Vohburg to Neustadt   15 or 14.2 km

🄵 From Vohburg you now have a choice of two routes to Neustadt a. d. Donau. One route takes you via Pförring along the north bank, the other takes you on mostly unpaved paths directly along the dike on the south bank.

North bank via Pförring   15 km

Ride over the bridge across the Danube ～ then right on **Schützenstraße** ～ and onto the

Kleines Donautor, Vohburg

bike path next to the road to Dünzing.

Dünzing

Stay on the main street though the town and continue towards Wackerstein.

Wackerstein

Turn left as you reach the village and ride along **Vohburger Straße** ～ continue until you reach **Vohburger Straße** on the ohter side of the village ～ **3** turn left, then keep right and follow the road to Pförring ～ you entre the town along the **Ingolstädter Straße**.

Pförring

Postal Code: 85104; Area code: 08403

- ℹ️ **Tourism office**, Marktpl. 1, ✆ 1528
- ✴️ **Roman fort "Celeusum"**, 1 km north of town

4 Turn right at the T-intersection ～ after crossing the bridge follow the **Donaustraße** for a short distance ～ turn left and follow the street **Geisgries** ～ you pass a lake as you

leave Pförring ～ cross straight over the main road and continue to the dike along the river ～ turn left and follow the path along the dike ～ go through the underpass below the **B 299** main road ～ keep left ～ cross the street and follow the bicycle path to the left ～ by the T-intersection cross to the bicycle path on the other side of the street and follow this path along the left side of the **B 299** across the bridge ～ on the other bank continue straight ahead on the bicycle path **5**. Here the two routes rejoin.

🄰 Here you have the option of taking a much shorter alternative route which bypasses the towns of Neustadt and Bad Gögging and follows an unpaved path beside the creeks Ilm and Abens. The route is reached by turning sharply to the left and following the gravel road under the bidge to the Danube.

To take the main route, follow the bicycle path to the left into **Neustadt a. d. Donau** ～ continue until you reach the turnoff to Bad Gögging. The centre of Neustadt lies straight ahead.

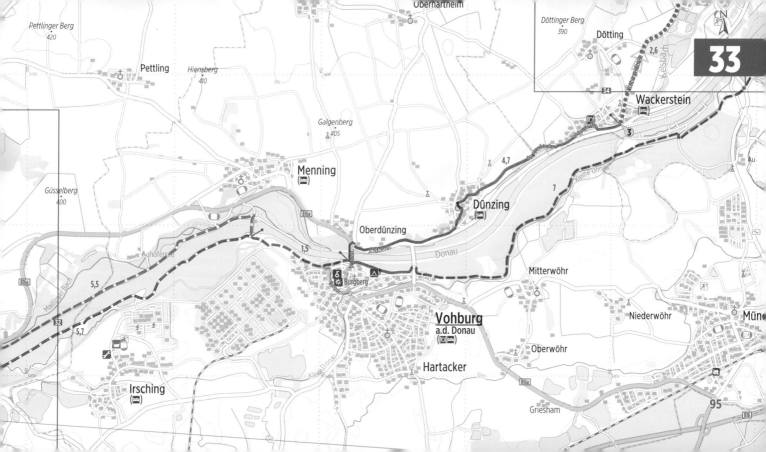

Pettlinger Berg
420

Pettling

Hiensberg
410

Obernartheim

Döttinger Berg
390

Dötting

2,6

Kelsbach

CN

Wackerstein

34

3

Galgenberg
405

Menning

4,7

Kleine Donau

7

Au

Dünzing

B16a

Oberdünzing

Güsselberg
400

Auhofersee

1,5

Donau

Mitterwöhr

Maillinger Bach

5,5

B16a

5,7

Burgberg

Burgberg

Vohburg
a.d. Donau

Niederwöhr

Mün

Oberwöhr

Irsching

Kleine Donau

Hartacker

Ilm

Griesham

B16a

B16

95

South bank along the dike   *14.2 km*

Cross the road leading to the bridge and take the first side street ~ turn left out to the dike and follow the path below the dike ~ you pass below the road bridge ~ continue along the dike, which follows the Kleine Donau (Little Danube) ~ after about 4 km you cross the little bridge and continue along the other bank ~ cross the road and continue along the path ~ you pass the village of **Gaden** and continue to the large road bridge.

ALTERNATIVE Here you have the option of continuing straight ahead, following the unpaved path beside the creeks Ilm and Abens. This route is much shorter, but bypasses the towns of Neustadt and Bad Gögging.

To follow the main route turn right just before the bridge ~ immediately turn left and ride under the bridge ~ after the right bend continue straight ahead onto the bicycle path **5**. Here the two main routes rejoin.

Follow the bicycle path to the left into Neustadt a. d. Donau ~ continue until you reach the turnoff to Bad Gögging. The centre of Neustadt lies straight ahead.

Neustadt a. d. Donau

Postal Code: 93333; Area code: 09445

🛈 **Tourist Information,** Bad Gögging, ✆ 0800/46344464 or 95750, www.bad-goegging.de

🕒 **St. Andreas church**

✎ **Fahrrad Weigl,** Herderstr. 7, ✆ 2468

✎ **Müller,** Rambaldistr. 3, ✆ 7960

Between Neustadt and Eining you will find yourself riding through a major hops growing area. The tall trellises supporting the rapidly growing plants have virtually attained landmark status in this part of Bavaria.

Neustadt to Kelheim   *18 km*

Turn left into the **Bad Gögginger Straße** (St 2233) ~ a bicycle path begins as you leave Neustadt and ends as you reach Bad Gögging ~ continue straight ahead along the main street into the centre, where you cross the river Abens.

Bad Gögging

Postal Code: 93333; Area code: 09445

🛈 **Tourist Information,** Heiligenstädter Str. 5, ✆ 0800/46344464 or 95750, www.bad-goegging.de

🏛 **Roman baths museum,** in the St. Andreas church, Trajansstr. 8, Open: Mar.-Oct., Tue-Sun 16-17.

✱ **Fisheries educational trail**

🗕 **Limes Baths Resort,** modern therapy centre with sulfur, moor and thermal spas ✆ 20090.

✎ 🚲 **Rad'l Reger,** Heiligenstädter Str. 9, ✆ 1058

Continue along the main street, now called **Römerstraße**, to Sittling.

Sittling

In the village turn left in the right bend ~ keep right at the fork and follow street out of the village ~ continue straight at the crossing and ride over the river Abends ~ turn right immediately after the bridge ~ follow the dike path to Eining ~ turn right across the bridge into Eining.

Eining

✱ **Roman castrum Abusina,** Abusinastr. 16, Open: free access, free entry. Open-air museum with excavations of one of the largest Roman Roman military settlements in Bavaria, information boards, viewing platform.

After the bridge turn right to the main street ~ turn right and immediately left into the

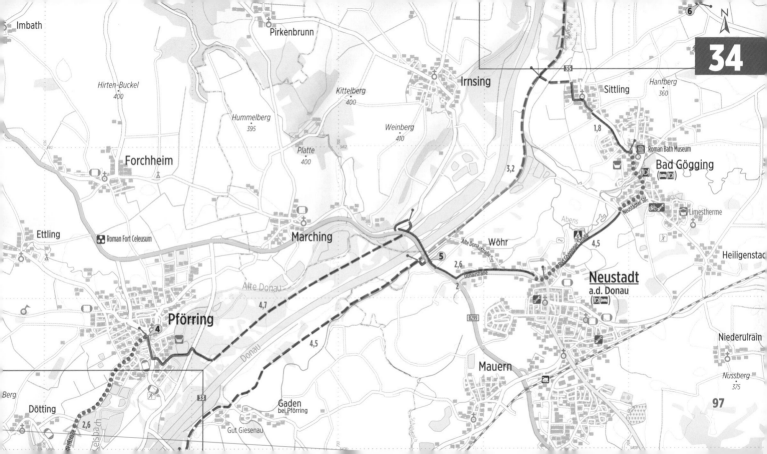

Imbath

Pirkenbrunn

Hirten-Buckel
400

Hummelberg
395

Kittelberg
400

Irnsing

Sittling

Hanfberg
360

Forchheim

Platte
400

Weinberg
410

1,8

Roman Bath Museum

Bad Gögging

3,2

Limestherme

Ettling

Roman Fort Celeusum

Marching

Wöhr

Alte Donaustraße

5

2,6

Donaustraße

Neustadt a.d.Str.

Bad Gögginger Straße

4,5

Heiligenstac

Abens

Neustadt
a.d. Donau

Alte Donau

4,7

2

Niederulrain

Pförring

4

B299

Donau

4,5

Mauern

Nussberg
375

Berg

33

Dötting

2,6

Gaden
bei Pförring

Gut Giesenau

street **Pfarrer-Krottenthaler-Straße** ～ as you leave Eining continue on the bicycle path along the road ～ **6** turn left by the brickworks ～ continue to the intersection at the end of the paved road. From here you can see the church at Sandharlanden ～ go left and climb a few more meters elevation ～ you can catch your breath on the descent down to Staubing ～ and enjoy the fine views into the Danube valley ～ keep right into **Flecksteinstraße** at the fork as you reach the first houses of Staubing ～ follow the left bend onto the **Holzharlander Weg** ～ you pass under the main road.

Weltenburg Abbey

Staubing

In Staubing keep right on the street **Ortsring** ～ take the street **Am Krautgarten** to the right out of the village ～ turn left before reaching the main road and ride down to the Danube ～ follow the path to the right along the Danube ～ **7** after the playing fields you either turn right to connect with the alternative route to Kelheim or continue straight ahead to **Asamstraße**, where you turn right to reach the Abbey and the ferry.

Weltenburg

- 🛈 **Weltenburg Benedictine Abbey**, Bavaria's oldest abbey was founded in 610 AD. The current buildings were erected in the 18th c. by the Asam brothers.
- ⛴ **Passenger ship service between Weltenburg and Kelheim**, Kelheim office, ☏ 09441/5858.
- ⛴ **Wooden boots** also ply the river between Weltenburg and Kelheim.

The boat Kelheim in the Danube gorge

The magnificent Weltenburg Abbey is believed to be the oldest monastery in Bavaria. The ceiling frescoes in the abbey church of the venerable old complex were created by the brothers Cosmas Damian and Egid Quirin Asam and are considered masterworks of baroque design. It depicts a heavenly Jerusalem soaring above the church nave and is so perfectly executed that the viewer cannot see transitions in the decoration.

ALTERNATIVE The official bicycle route takes a steep and busy road up the mountain and then follows a rough forest track, bypassing much of the dramatic scenery as the Danube winds its way through the Franconian Jura. We therefore recommend you board an excursion boat or wooden barge at Weltenburg and enjoy the views from the water on the 5 km trip to Kelheim. Regardless of whether you take the boat or battle the traffic over the mountain, we strongly urge you to take a break at the Weltenburg Abbey and sample what the monks have done with the local hops.

TIP The boats down the river depart from pontoons just downstream from the abbey. The passage to Kelheim takes about 20 minutes.

The Danube gorge

The boat that shuttles between Weltenburg and Kelheim passes through a narrow valley of overwhelming beauty. It has taken eons for the river to carve this narrow path through the Franconian Jura ridge. The result is a winding narrow gorge of white cliffs that rise from beneath the river's surface to heights of almost 100 meters, and reduce the river's width to less than 70 meters.

The way in which the bizarre shapes of the rocks seem to push and shove each other and change shapes as the boat passes has inspired river travelers to give them names and invent fantastic stories about the gorge. There are the "three brothers" who turned to stone when two

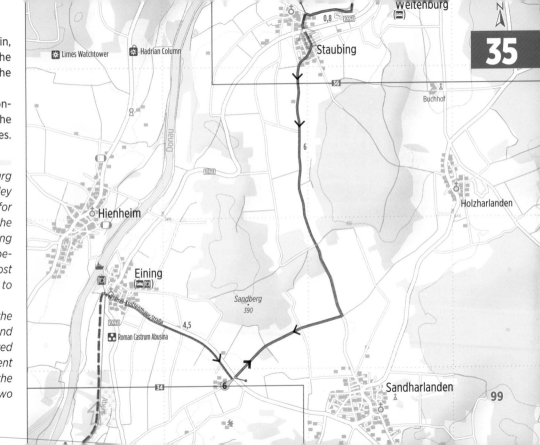

By Weltenburg

of them attempted to drown the third in the Danube's waters. There is the "stone pulpit" from which Luther is said to have preached to the fishermen, plus a "Bavarian lion" and the "pious bishop" who prays for the souls of the monks at Weltenburg.

In addition to these nature-made spectacles, the gorge offers cultural highlights, especially Weltenburg Abbey, which is said to be the oldest in Bavaria. It was founded in the year 610 by Columban monks. The brothers Cosmas Damian and Egid Quirin Asam helped build the current structures and painted the famous ceiling frescoes in the abbey church.

Hall of liberation

At the end of the spectacular ride through the gorge there is another impressive edifice on a bluff above the river just upstream from Kelheim. It is the Hall of Liberation, or Befreiungshalle, commissioned by King Ludwig I and built by Leo von Klenze, who was also responsible for the Hall of Fame, or Walhalla, a few kilometers further downstream. The Befreiungshalle was erected in memory of those who contributed to Germany's liberation from Napoleon's rule. Inside the circular structure stand eighteen oversized winged angels holding hands.

TIP In the lower Altmühl valley between Kelheim und Dietfurt you have the opportunity to take a trip into the past in Bavaria's largest archaeo-logical park. Numerous sculptures and replicas placed in 18 different locations can be explored on foot or by bicycle. Detailed information is available in the Tourist-Information Kehlheim. The stations which are covered in map 36 have been marked with purple numbers (Point **1** in Kelheim).

Kelheim, hall of liberation

Kelheim

Postal Code: 93309; Area code: 09441

🛈 **Tourist-Information**, Ludwigspl. 1, ✆ 701234, www.kelheim.de

🚢 **Passenger ship sevice on the Main-Donau canal**, ✆ 5858, Scheduled service between Kelheim-Essing-Riedenburg-Dietfurt-Beilngries vom 23rd Apr.-16th Oct.

🚢 **Passenger ship sevice on the Danube**, Kelheim office ✆ 5858, Scheduled service between Kelheim and Weltenburg from 2st Mar.-1st Nov.

🏛 **Archaeological Museum**, Ledererg. 11, ✆ 10492, Open: Apr.-Oct., Tue-Sun 10-17. Documents early history of the lower Altmühl valley and the city of Kelheim in the middle ages.

🏛 **Befreiungshalle (Hall of Liberation)** on the Michelsberg, ✆ 68207-10, Open: 15th Mar.-Oct. 9-18, Nov.-15th Mar., 9-16.

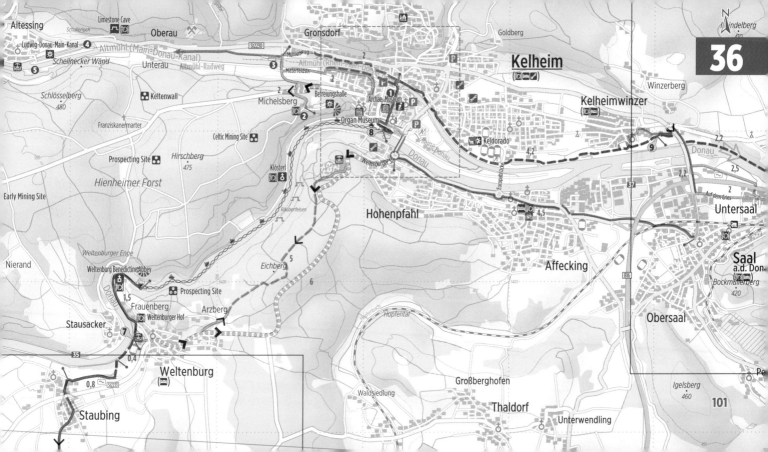

Limestone Cave

Schüllerloch

Oberau

Ludwig-Donau-Main-Kanal

Schellnecker Wänd

Unterau

Altmühl (Main-Donau-Kanal)

Altmühl-Radweg

Schlösselberg
480

Keltenwall

Franziskanermarter

Prospecting Site

Hirschberg
475

Hienheimer Forst

Celtic Mining Site

Early Mining Site

Michelsberg

Klösterl

Räuberfelsen

Weltenburger Enge

Nierand

Weltenburg Benedictine Abbey

Prospecting Site

Donau

1,5

Frauenberg

Weltenburger Hof

Stausacker

7

0,4

35

0,8

Staubing

Weltenburg

Eichberg

Arzberg

Gronsdorf

Mühlenweg

Mitterfeldstr.

Befreiungshalle

Organ Museum

Archä. Museum

Weltenburger St.

Hohenpfahl

5

6

Waldsiedlung

Hopfental

Thaldorf

Unterwendling

Goldberg

Kelheim

Keldorado

4,2

Main-Donau

Donau

Europakanäle

4,5

Affecking

Großberghofen

Igelsberg
460

Kelheimwinzer

Winzerberg

9

37

2,2

2,2

2,5

2

Auf dem Gries

Untersaal

Saal
a.d. Don.

Bockmühlberg
420

Obersaal

Pe

N

K=indelberg

101

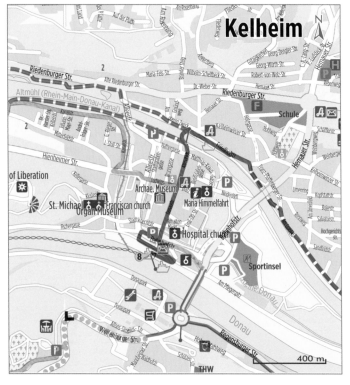

Kelheim

Imposing monument in memory of the Napoleonic Wars 1813-1815.

🏛 **Organ museum** in the Franciscan church, ☎ 5508, Open: Apr.-Oct., Tue-Sun 14-17, May-Sept., Thur. 8 pm, tours with concert.

🕎 **Maria Himmelfahrt parish church**, Kirchplatz. 15th c. gothic church with high altar made of Kelheim marble.

🕎 **Hospital church (Spitalkirche) & Otto chapel**, Wittelbachergasse. Romanesque church with baroque interior dating to 1231.

🕎 **Franciscan church**, Am Kirchensteig, ☎ 5508, Audio tours: Apr.-Oct., Tue-Sun 14-17. Abbey church with gothic and baroque frescoes from 1471-1803.

🏰 **Herzog palace**, Schlossweg. 12th century structure was modified in 1470 and today serves as local council seat.

✹ **Weißes Brauhaus (brew house)**, Emil-Ott-Str. 3-5, ☎ 3480. Brew house established in 1607 by Herzog Maximilian, has one of the prettiest beer gardens in Bavaria.

✹ **Keldorado**, Rennweg 60, ☎ 2267, Open: Summer: daily 9-20:30, Winter: Mon-Fri 9-21, Sat,

Sun 9-20. Swimming and recreational complex.

♨ **Bicycle storage boxes** available at the ship landings for Danube and Altmühl, and in the town hall courtyard.

🚲 **Bike Station**, Kelheimwinzerstr. 101, ☎ 179880

🚲 **2 Rad Jessen**, Schäfflerstr. 12, ☎ 504850

🚲 **Zweirad Center im Donaupark**, Donaupark 33, ☎ 3024

The origins of Kelheim can be found on the Michelsberg, a bluff on the peninsula formed by the Danube and the Altmühl rivers. In the fifth century BC this was the site of Alkmoenna, a Celtic city protected by earthen walls. Today the Hall of Liberation dominates the location. It was commissioned by King Ludwig I of Bavaria. Built from 1842 to 1863, its design recalls an ancient burial temple as well as the Pantheon in Rome. The inscription above the entrance reads "For the German Freedom

Fighters Ludwig I of Bavaria" and the Roman numerals MDCCCLXIII in memory of the date, October 18 1863, the Hall was opened. It was the 50th anniversary of the Battle of Leipzig.

Kelheim to Bad Abbach   16.5 km

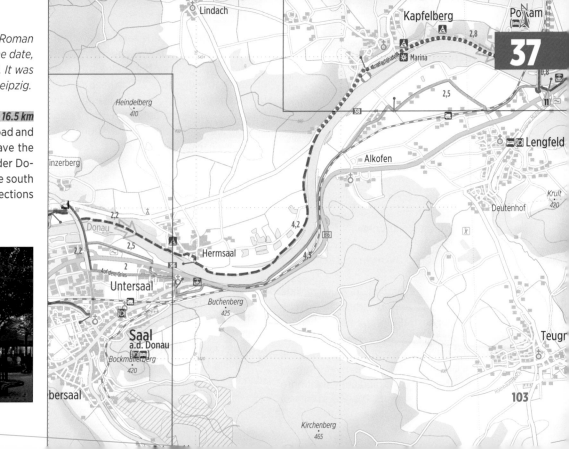

ALTERNATIVE If you arrive in Kehlheim along the road and do not wish to visit the city, you have the option of riding directly to Saal an der Donau and the alternative route along the south bank. The train station in Saal has connections to Regensburg and Ingolstadt.

Ludwigsplatz, Kelheim

103

South bank to Saal   4.5 km

Before crossing the bridge over the Danube, turn right at the roundabout and take the bicycle lane along the **Regensburger Straße** ~ straight by the roundabout at the next bridge ~ continue along the industrial area ~ under a road bridge and through the railway underpass ~ continue along **Kelheimer Straße** to the roundabout in Saal. From the roundabout turn left, third exit, into **Donaustraße** ~ straight across the railway crossing ~ turn right into the lane **Auf dem Gries** to connect with the alternative route along the south bank or continue straight ahead cross the bridge to the main route along the north bank.

8 From the ship landing in Kelheim ride into the historic centre ~ through the city gate on **Donaustraße** ~ the name changes to **Altmühlstraße** at the town hall ~ continue 200 m to another city gate ~ take the pedestrian bridge over the river Altmühl ~ turn left and then immediately right onto

Friedhofstraße ~ and ride next to the Altmühl ~ turn right on **Franz-Pfaffenberger Straße** ~ after passing under the bridge turn right on **Am Grabfeld** ~ after 250 m keep right on the bicycle path and follow the dike along the Danube ~ you pass below another bridge as you leave Kelheim ~ you soon reach Kelheimwinzer.

Kelheimwinzer

CENTRE To ride through the centre of Kelheimwinzer, turn left between the playing field and the church.

Along **Pfarrer Plaß Weg** ~ turn right on **Dorfring** ~ after the left curve turn right and immediately right again into **Herrnsaaler Weg** ~ after 300 m you reach the pumping station on the dike **9**.

Continue to the pumping station on the dike at the far end of Kelheimwinzer **9**.

ALTERNATIVE Here you have the opportunity to change to the route along the south bank, thus avoiding the heavy traffic along the main road by Kapfelberg and Poikam.

South bank alternative
to Bad Abbach   12.5 km

Keep left and take the path up onto the bridge ~ after crossing the Danube keep left and follow the path down to a small street ~ turn right and ride past the wastewater treatment plant ~ after the underpass you entre the village **Untersaal** ~ turn left ~ at the end of the street left onto the street **Auf dem Gries** ~ cross the **Regensburger Straße** into **Bachgasse** ~ turn left after the small bridge and follow the street out of Untersaal ~ after passing under the main road you come to ride along the Danube ~ at the intersection near **Alkofen** continue on **Mitterfeldstraße** beside the railway line ~ follow the street through the village, then between fields and scattered farms ~ turn left after the bridge across the railway line ~ this street takes you parallel to the railway line back to the Danube ~ turn left and ride under the bridge across the barrage ~ **11** a bicycle path begins to the right immediately after the bridge. You are now on the main route to Bad Abbach.

To take the main route along the north bank from Kelheimwinzer, **9** continue straight along the dike past the pumping station ⌇ turn right after passing under the bridge and follow the gravel path along the Danube to Hermsaal ⌇ keep right by the houses, then right again at the T-intersection ⌇ after a short distance turn right and continue on the path along the river bank until you reach the main road ⌇ here you must ride with the traffic to Kapfelberg ⌇ turn right after the playing field onto **Am Yachthafen** ⌇ follow the road past the Marina and along the Danube to Poikam.

Poikam

After the left bend you reach an intersection by the railway underpass **10** ⌇ turn right into **Dorfstraße** and ride through the underpass ⌇ continue to the next 4-way intersection.

ALTERNATIVE To bypass Bad Abbach on a slightly shorter alternative route past the **Inselbad** outdoor pool, turn left here and follow **Kreuzstraße** out of Poikam, then straight across the main

road and the canal to the pedestrian and bicycle bridge over the Danube **12**.

Otherwise turn right and ride to the main road ~ turn right again and ride over the bridge across the Danube ~ turn right at the end of the bridge ~ then right again to pass under the bridge ~ **11** a bicycle path begins to the right immediately after the bridge.

Follow the bicycle path beside the main road, then along the river bank to Bad Abbach.

CENTRE | To ride via the city centre, turn right into the paved path to the underpass under the main road, then left along **Kaiser-Karl-V.-Allee**, through the pedestrian zone, then straight ahead before turning right through the underpass towards **Oberndorf**.

Bad Abbach

Postal Code: 93077; Area code: 09405

- 🛈 **Resort offices**, Kaiser-Karl-V.-Allee 5, 📞 95990
- 🏛 **Museum Bad Abbach**, Rathaus, Raiffeisenstr. 72, 📞 95900, Open: Sun 14-16.
- ✸ **Heinrichsturm/Hungerturm**. 27 m tower from 1200-1229.
- 📷 **Kaiser-Therme**, Kurallee 4, 📞 95170

- ✉ **Inselbad outdoor pool**, Inselbadstr. 2a, 📞 940623, Open: May-Sept., daily 9-20.

Bad Abbach to Regensburg　　　*21.7 km*

The main route follows the path along the river through Bad Abbach ~ **12** continue under the pedestrian and bicycle bridge ~ turn left on the main road ~ after 750 m turn right into the gravel path along the dike past **Oberndorf** ~ by the main road continue on the paved bicycle path, which takes you along the bank of the Danube to Matting.

Steinerne Brücke, Regensburg,

Matting

Postal Code: 93080; Area code: 0941

- ⚓ **Historic Reaction ferry**, 📞 92082-13

After the ferry landing continue to the left along the street past the playing field ~ follow the bicycle path along the river bank, which becomes unpaved after the inn ~ **13** you pass below a road bridge and then a railway bridge as you reach **Großprüfening** ~ continue downstream on the gravel bicycle path along the river bank ~ stay on the path through the Donaupark ~ you pass under a large road bridge, the A93 freeway ~ continue past the Herzogspark ~ straight ahead along the **Holzländstraße** ~ you come to ride in heavy traffic, continue straight on **Am Weinmarkt**, **Keplerstraße** and **Fischmarkt**, until you reach the old Stone Bridge (Steinerne Brücke). **1**

TIP | You are now in the centre of one of the most impressive cities of Europe. Take time to explore the medieval streets and alleys of Regensburg's extensive historic centre, which boasts a great variety of impressive historic architecture.

Regensburg

Postal Code: 93047; Area code: 0941

🛈 **Tourismusinfo**, Landratsamt Regensburg, Altmühlstr. 1, ☎ 4009-495, www.landkreis-regensburg.de

🛈 **Tourist-Information**, Altes Rathaus, Rathauspl. 4, ☎ 5074410, www.regensburg.de

⚓ **Regensburger Personenschifffahrt Klinger GmbH**, ☎ 52104, Operates: Apr.-Oct., River cruises on the Danube.

⚓ **Donauschifffahrt Wurm & Köck**, ☎ 50277880, Operates: Apr.-Oct., River cruises on the Danube.

🏛 **Diocese museum St. Ulrich**, Dompl. 2, ☎ 597-2530, Open: 1st Apr.-1st Nov., Tue-Sun 10-17. Collection includes sculptures, paintings, works of bronze and gold.

🏛 **Diocese museum Obermünster**, Emmeramspl. 1, ☎ 597-2530, Open by arrangement. Religious art and folk art, library and photo archive.

🏛 **Cathedral treasure museum**, Krauterermarkt 3, ☎ 597-2530, Open: 1st Apr.-1st Nov., Tue-Sat 10-17, Sun/Hol 12-17. Gold and other jewels and treasures from the 11th-20th c.

🏛 **Thurn und Taxis palace and cloister St. Emmeram**, Emmeramspl. 5, ☎ 5048-133, Tours: Apr.-Oct., daily, hourly 11:30-16:30, Nov.-Mar., Sat, Sun/Hol 10:30, 11:30, 13:30, 14:30, 15:30. Main attractions are furnishings from the former palais in Brussels and the residence in Frankfurt.

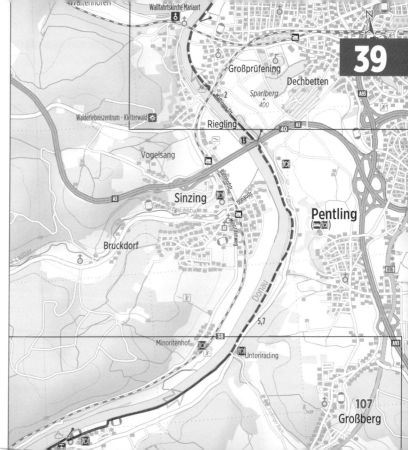

39

107
Großberg

🏛 **Thurn und Taxis Museum: Princely treasury**, Emmeramspl. 5, ✆ 5048-133, Open: Apr.-Oct., Mon-Fri 11-17, Sat, Sun/Hol. 10-17, Nov.-Mar., Sat, Sun/Fei 10-17. Fine furniture, porcelain, exclusive gold and silver items, an unique collection snuff tabacco boxes and numerous other precious items which testify to the glory of one of Europe's leading nobility. The royal stables museum (**Marstallmuseum**) shows coaches, sleds, sedan chairs, saddles and other riding accessories. Open upon request.

🏛 **Kepler Memorial House**, Keplerstr. 5, ✆ 5073442, Open: Sat, Sun/Hol 10:30-16, Tours: Sat, Sun/Hol. 14:30 and by arrangement. Exhibits covering the life and work of the famous astronomer and mathematician.

🏛 **Museum of History**, Dachaupl. 2-4, ✆ 507-2448, Open: Tues, Weds, Fri-Sun/Hol 10-16, Thur 10-20. Documents the art and art history of Regensburg and Eastern Bavaria.

🏛 **Reichstagmuseum in the Altes Rathaus**, ✆ 507-3440, Tours: Apr.-Oct., daily 9:30, 10, 10:30, 11, 11:30, 12, 13:30, 14, 14:30, 15(engl.), 15:30, 16, Nov.-Jan. & Mar., daily 10, 11:30, 13:30, 14(engl.), 15, 15:30, Jan.-Feb., daily 10, 11:30, 13:30, 15. Documents the history of the parliamentary sessions in Regensburg.

🏛 **Danube shipping museum**, Thundorfer Straße, Marc-Aurel-Ufer, ✆ 5075888, Open: Apr.-Oct., Tue-Sun 10-17. Museum on the paddle steam tug Ruthof, built in 1922 and similar to the "Maria-Anna" type ships used on the Danube since 1837.

🏛 **document Neupfarrplatz**. Dachaupl. 2-4, ✆ 5071442. Underground information centre at Neupfarrplatz about Roman times, medieval Jewish quarter, early modernity and Nazi period. Guided tours only: Thur-Sat 14:30, July/Aug, Thur-Mon 14:30, tickets at ✆ 54831.

🏛 **Brückturm Museum**, Weiße-Lamm-G. 1, ✆ 5075889. Open: Apr.-Oct., Tue-Sun 10-17. Objects and information about the history of the Steinerne Brücke and shipping on the Danube.

🏛 **Eastern Bavaria natural history museum**, am Prebrunntor 4, ✆ 507-3443, Open: Mon 9-12, Tue-Fri 9-16, Sun 10-17. Exhibits about the geology and landscape of Eastern Bavaria.

🏛 **City Gallery "Leeren Beutel"**, Bertoldstr. 9, ✆ 5072440, Open: Tue-Sun 10-16. 20th c. Eastern Bavarian art, ongoing special exhibitions of modern art.

🏛 **Artforum Eastern German Gallery**, Dr.-Johann-Maier-Str. 5, ✆ 297140, Open: Tue, Wed, Fri-Sun 10-17, Thur 10-20. Paintings, prints and sculpture by Eastern European artists from the 19th and 20th c.

🏛 **Golf museum**, Tändlerg. 3 (Antikhaus Insam), ✆ 51074, Open: Mon-Sat 10-18.

🏛 **document Niedermünster**, Niedermünsterg. 4, Guided tours only: May-Oct., Mon,

Sun/Hol. 14:30, Information and registration at **Infozentrum DOMPLATZ 5**, Dompl. 5, ✆ 597-1660. One of the laregst archaeological excavations in Germany lies below the Romanesque Niedermünster Church from the 12th c.

🗙 **St. Peter's cathedral**, Info centre, Dompl. 5, ✆ 5971660, Open: Apr.-Oct., 6:30 & 18:00, Nov.-Mar., 6:30-17. With bishops graves, cloister and all saints chapel.

🗙 **Basilika u. l. Frau zur Alten Kapelle**, Alten Kornmarkt. Built in 875, it was renovated in the mid 18th c., becomeing one of the most opulent Rococo churches in Bavaria.

✪ **Guided bike tours**, for further information contact Regensburger Tourismus GmbH and ✆ 507-3413 and -3417

✪ **Steinerne Brücke (Stone bridge)** (12th c.) with **Brücktor (Bridge gate)** (14th c.)

✪ **Porta Praeoria**, Fischmarkt, Regensburg's oldest city gate, built by the Romans around 179 AD.

✪ **Welterbe (world heritage) Regensburg visitor's centre in the Salzstadel**, Weisse-Lamm-G. 1, ✆ 5075410, Open: daily 10-19.

🏞 **Botanic garden**, University, Open: Mon 7-16, Thur 7-15:30, Fri 7-14 & -Sun 11-18. By good weather in winter.

Regensburg, Porta Praetoria

40

Tremmelhauserhöhe

Wutzlhofen

Kareth

Rehthal

Gallingkofen

Konradsiedlung

Brandlberg
415

Grubberg
490

Kühbuckel
445

Niederwinzer

Sallern

Geological Trail

Oberwinzer

Steinweg

Reinhausen

Schwabelweis

Kager

Frankenstr.

Weichs

Kneiting

Donaupark

Schleusenkanal

Schwabelweiserweg
4,5

Donau

Westbad

1,8

Holzländestr.

Steinerne Brücke

1,5

Regensburg

Hüpberg
400

Herzogspark

Kepler Memorial House

Kepler...

Shipping Museum
Eiserne Brücke

0,4

4,2

Prüfening

1

St. Peter's

Mariaort

Museum of History

kirche Mariaort

Fürst Thurn und Taxis palace museum

Maximilianstr.

Irlmauth

Großprüfening

Königswiesen

Karthaus

Dechbetten

Sparlberg
400

2

Riegling

Steinerne Brücke and Cathedral, Regensburg

- ➕ **Reptile Zoo**, Obertraublinger Str. 25, Open: 10-18.
- 🚲 **Rent a Bike**, Bahnhofstr. 18, Infohotline ✆ 5998808, Service, rental, repairs, sales.
- 🚲 **Zweirad Ehrl**, Am Protzenweiher 5-7, 85124, e-bikes
- 🚲 **Bikehaus Bikeambulanz**, Bahnhofstr. 18, west railway station building, ✆ 5998808
- 🚲 **Bikehaus**, Landshuter Str. 19, ✆ 46520781
- 🚲 **Stadler**, Kirchmeierstr. 22, ✆ 37880
- 🚲 **Stadler**, Schäffnerstr. 25-29, ✆ 51246
- 🚲 **Fahrrad Rosenhammer**, Lappersdorfer Str. 2, ✆ 84223
- 🚲 **Love Hurts**, Hofgartenweg 10, ✆ 5041437
- 🚲 **Feine Räder**, Furtmayrstr. 10-12, ✆ 7000365
- 🚲 **Fahrrad Werkstatt**, Reiterstr. 28, ✆ 2066620

Regensburg is an interesting city. Its history goes back more than 2,000 years, and few old cities can boast as many surviving medieval buildings and structures. The Steinerne Brücke, or Stone Bridge, for instance, is not only the oldest functioning bridge over the Danube, but the oldest bridge in Germany. It was commissioned by Duke Henry the Proud and built in the first half of the 12th century.

Johann Wolfgang Goethe observed that in Regensburg "churches stand upon churches", but there are many other significant buildings as well. The old city with its narrow cobbled streets and impressive old homes, church buildings and the Thurn und Taxis palace has been designated a world heritage site by UNESCO. Numerous city squares, alleyways and markets, the colourful houses and old towers and gates give Regensburg a certain Mediterranean flair, which is why the city on the Danube is sometimes referred to as "the northernmost city of Italy."

The city's most distinctive landmark is the cathedral. The earliest parts of the church date to the 8th century and in 1255 the city began erecting a gothic structure. Construction was halted due to a lack of funds in 1525, and the cathedral was not completed until the 19th century. The northside of the building includes the so-called Eselsturm (donkey's tower), a romanesque element.

Regensburg was also the hometown of the astronomer and mathematician Johannes Kepler. The house at Keplerstraße 5, where he lived and died, has been converted into a museum. While Galileo Galilei was being forced to recant his theories about the motions of the planets, Kepler was allowed to publish his works unhindered – even though his mother had been accused of witchcraft.

Goldener Turm, Regensburg

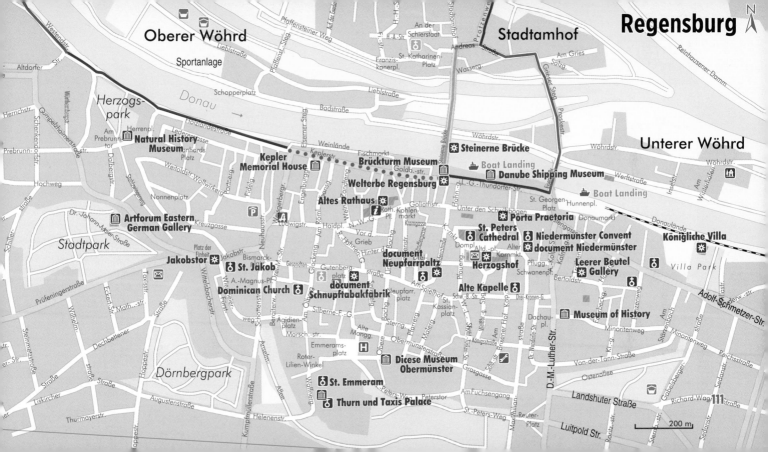

Regensburg

Oberer Wöhrd

Sportanlage

Donau

Stadtamhof

Unterer Wöhrd

Herzogs-park

Natural History Museum

Kepler Memorial House

Brückturm Museum

Steinerne Brücke

Boat Landing

Danube Shipping Museum

Boat Landing

Welterbe Regensburg

Altes Rathaus

Artforum Eastern German Gallery

Stadtpark

Porta Praetoria

Königliche Villa

Villa Park

Jakobstor

St. Jakob

document Neupfarrplatz

St. Peters Cathedral

Niedermünster Convent

document Niedermünster

Leerer Beutel Gallery

Herzogshof

Dominican Church

document Schnupftabakfabrik

Alte Kapelle

Museum of History

Dörnbergpark

Diecese Museum Obermünster

St. Emmeram

Thurn und Taxis Palace

111

200 m

Regensburg to Passau 145.6 km

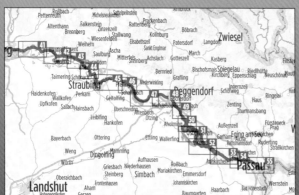

Downstream from Regensburg the Bohemian mountains force the Danube to turn to the southeast. The river passes along the northern edge of the fertile plain known in Germany as the Gäuboden while the foothills of the Bavarian Forest reach down to the river from the north. The river has grown in stature at this point and teems with ship traffic. The bike route heads downstream to Straubing, long considered the capital of the Gäuboden. The river meanders through graceful curves across the landscape until it reaches Deggendorf, gateway to the Bavarian Forest and the ancient rounded hills that rise towards the Czech border. The Danube bike route through Germany ends in "the Venice of the North," as the three-rivers city Passau likes to call itself. The city has a great deal to offer, ranging from the cathedral and catholic university to the old town hall, the pretty baroque city centre and the fortress standing guard on the bluff across the Danube.

The route follows mostly quiet country roads and bicycle paths, with only a few short stretches on busy roads.

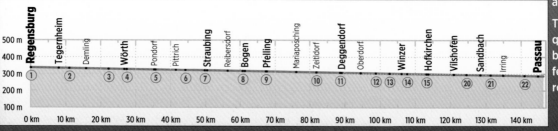

41

Keilberg

Donaustaufer Forst

Dachsberg
505

Hamerberg
480

Heiberg
520

Dachsberg

Donaustauf

Reiflding

Geological Trail

Tegernheim

Donaustauf Ruin

Chinese Tower

Walhalla

Sulzbach

Scheuchenberg
540

Schwabelweis

Donau

Neudemling

Baier Wine Museum

4,5

Demling

Friesheim

40

Sarching

Sarchinger See

nauth

Irl

Kreuzhof

Unterheising

Barbing

Steinbuckel
330

1 From the **Steinerne Brücke** go straight on the bike path on the left side of **Thundorfer Straße** ~ cross the Danube over the next bridge, the Eiserne Brücke ~ in the right bend, continue straight into **Proskestraße** and across the narrow bridge **Grieser Steg** ~ follow the **Andreasstraße** past the church ~ turn right at the T-intersection and cross the bridge **Protzenweiherbrücke** ~ at the next intersection turn right onto the bicycle path along **Frankenstraße** ~ after the bridge turn right into the first side street, **Holzgartenstraße** ~ after 500 m right on

View from Donaustauf Ruin

Bedelgasse ~ at the end of the narrow lane turn left under the road bridge and continue along **Johannisstraße** ~ left on **Weichser Weg** and immediately right on **Schwabelweiser Weg** ~ turn left and immediately right and follow the street away from the houses ~ you ride under a railway bridge and pass a large parking area ~ after passing under a large road bridge continue straight along **Schwabelweiser Donauufer** ~ at the end of the street keep right into the bicycle path ~ after passing wetlands continue straight on the street beside the dike past Tegernheim.

Tegernheim
Postal code: 93105; Area code: 09403

✿ Geopfad (geological trail) in the Tegernheim Gorge.

🔧 Fahrradservice Zdenko Francuski, Hauptstr. 44, ✆ 962330

Continue on the pleasant path along the dike to **Donaustauf**, where you can already see the famous Walhalla in the distance.

> **CENTRE** A bicycle and pedestrian bridge leads to the left across the busy main road, giving you easy access to the centre of Donaustauf.

The main route continues straight along the path parallel to the main road past Donaustauf

Walhalla

~ continue until you reach an underpass by the allotment gardens **2**.

> **EXCURSION** To reach Walhalla by bicycle you must make a long and steep climb. It is much easier to park your bicycle and use the footpath, which starts 500 m past the St. Salvator church and leads steeply up through the woods.

Donaustauf
Postal Code: 93093; Area code: 09403

🛈 Touristinfo Donaustauf, Maxstr. 24, ✆ 9552929, www.touristinfo-donaustauf.de

🏛 St. Salvator pilgrimage church, built in gothic style in the 15th c., then converted to baroque style before Leo von Klenze modified it in 1843 to complement Walhalla.

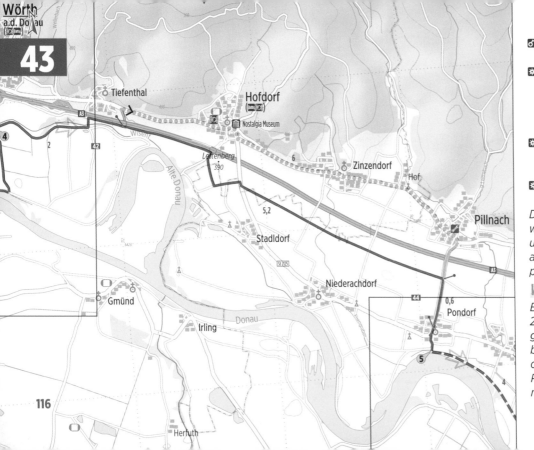

Tiefenthal

Hofdorf

Nostalgia Museum

Lottenberg
390

Zinzendorf

Hof

Stadldorf

Pillnach

Niederachdorf

Gmünd

Donau

Pondorf

Irling

Herfurth

116

Donaustauf ruin, defensive fortifications first built in 914 and destroyed by Swedish forces in 1634 during the Thirty Years War.

Walhalla, Walhalla-Str. 48, ☎ 961680, Open: Apr.-Sept., 9-17:45, Oct., 9-16:45, Nov.-Mar., 10-11:45 & 13-15:45. Commissioned by King Ludwig I and built by Leo von Klenze 1830-42. Doric-style temple is the most important classical German structure of the 19th c.

Chinese tower. The tower was moved from the Donaustauf palace garden to the Prüfenring palace garden in Regensburg in 1900. In 1999 it was returned to the Donaustaufen site.

Historic centre. Consists mainly of late-classicist buildings, which wrap around the base of the castle mountain.

Donaustauf is a picturesque little town that wraps around the base of a small mountain under the ruins of the old castle. It emerged as a market town in the middle ages under the protection of the then mighty fortifications.

Walhalla

Even as Bavarian crown prince at the age of 20, Ludwig I wanted to build a temple to honor great Germans. But he had to wait 19 years before he could lay the cornerstone for Walhalla on the Bräuberg near Donaustauf not far from Regensburg. He had already commissioned 60 marble busts for the site.

When it finally opened in October 1842, there were 162 figures honored in the building. A few years later Ludwig I built the Hall of Liberation near Kelheim.

The two monuments were built by the same architect, Leo von Klenze, who modelled Walhalla on the Parthenon in Athens. 348 marble steps lead up to the entrance. The temple's walls and columns are also made of marble, and the dimensions of the interior spaces almost exactly match those of the Parthenon. The name Walhalla comes from an old Nordic legend. "Walhall" is the place where the God of Gods and Battles, Odin (also known as Wotan) welcomes fallen heroes to his table. In his last will and testament, Ludwig left instructions for new deserving Germans to be added to the Hall of Fame when fitting. It is a wish that the state government of Bavaria has honored at least 9 times since 1945.

Continue beside the main road past **Sulzbach** ~ at the end of the path turn right and continue along the river bank past **Demling** to Bach, which lies to the left away from the river.

Bach a. d. Donau

Postal Code: 93090; Area code: 09403

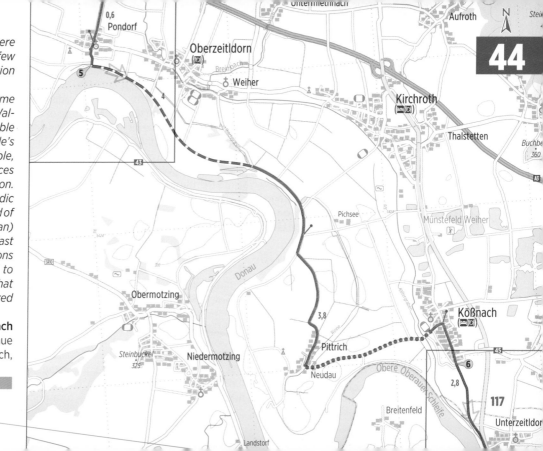

- 🏛 **Historic gemstone mine Kittenrain**, Am Kittenrain, ☎ 9529531, Open: Mar.-Oct., daily 11-17. Underground mine museum and exhibition mine.
- 🏛 **Baier Wine Museum**, Info: Wörther Str. 5 (Donaustauf), ☎ 95020, Open: May-Sept., Sun 13-16. Historic presshouse from the 14th c. and wine educational trail.

Continue along the river bank to Frengkofen.

Frengkofen

From here you ride on the road along the river ~ **3** you pass below a road bridge as you reach Kiefenholz.

Here the route divides. The southern route takes you along the Danube, partly on an unpaved path while the northern route takes you directly towards Wörth.

Along the Danube   9.7 km

To take the southern route turn right onto the unpaved path after passing under the freeway ~ ride beside the Danube ~ in the left bend after the sluices continue straight ahead into the upaved path ~ you pass below another road bridge ~ after another 4 km turn left opposite a wood ~ **4** at the T-intersection the two routes rejoin. Here you turn right to continue, to take the excursion to Wörth turn left and right at the next turnoff.

Short route via Kiefenholz   5 km

To take the northern route, after passing under the freeway follow the street into **Kiefenholz** ~ turn left opposite the church ride out of the village ~ continue straight ahead through the roundabout, using the bicycle path along the left side of the road ~ at the end of the bicycle path take the side road ~ keep right at the fork ~ continue straight across the road and along the dike.

To reach the Wörth an der Donau, turn left into the third side road over the dike

Wörth

Postal Code: 93086; Area code: 09482

- ℹ **Tourism office**, Rathauspl. 1, ☎ 94030
- ⛪ **St. Peter parish church**. 13th c. three-nave gothic basilica.
- 🏛 **Nostalgie Museum**, Zur Alten Donau 4, Wörth-Hofdorf, ☎ 90086, Open: Good Friday-3rd Oct., Sat, Sun/Hol 14-18.
- 🏰 **Wörth palace**, only the gate building, towers and keep of the medieval complex are still standing.
- 🔧 **FIAT Karlheinz Schneider**, Marktpl. 10, ☎ 94120

Wörth to Straubing   22.9 km

The main route continues straight ahead on the road along the dike **4** ~ turn left over the next bridge across the Wisent ~ turn right

Theresienplatz in Straubing

and continue parallel to the freeway ~ pass the first underpass ~ by the next underpass, take the path up at an angle to the right into the fields ~ left at the T-intersection and ride to the street ~ turn right and immediately left and follow the paved field road until you reach the third paved crossroad ~ turn right and ride into Pondorf.

Pondorf

Turn left in the village after the church and ride to the river ~ **5** turn left and follow the unpaved path along the dike ~ after about 3 km continue on the paved road to **Pitttrich** ~ turn left across the bridge and ride to Kößnach ~ you cross a dike and a waterway ~ continue straight to the T-intersection.

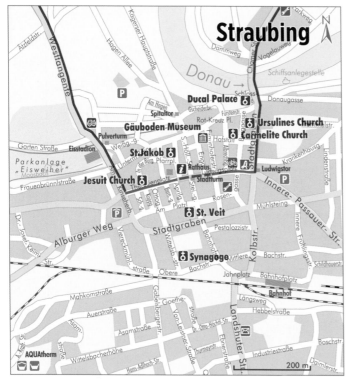

Straubing

Kößnach

Turn right on **Straubinger Straße** ~ **6** continue straight ahead into the paved lane at the end of the village ~ you come to ride beside the main road and through an underpass before reaching Sossau.

Sossau

🏛 Assumption of Maria pilgrimage church. Straight ahead along the street to the bridge.

If you do not wish to ride through Straubing you can take the shortcut along the dike to Hornstorf from here. Ride straight ahead on the path along the dike, which is unpaved by Hornstorf, and rejoin the main route coming from the bridge.

To ride through Straubing, turn right across the bridge, then left onto the bicycle path along the road ~ you cross the barrage on the Danube and come into Straubing ~ continue along the bicycle path past the **Straubinger**

Eisstadion ~ **7** by the second set of traffic lights turn left onto **Theresienplatz,** in the historic centre of the city.

Straubing

Postal Code: 94315; Area code: 09421

🛈 **Tourism office**, Theresienpl. 2, ☎ 944307, www.straubing.de

⚓ **Donau-Personenschifffahrt**, Reederei Wurm, Passau. Passenger ship service to Passau. ☎ 0851/929292

🏛 **Gäuboden Museum**, Fraunhoferstr. 23, ☎ 974110, Open: Tue-Sun 10-16. Includes the world-famous Straubing Roman treasure found in 1950 and items from the Bavarii, as well as local history and special exhibitions.

🏛 **St. Jakob Basilica**. Papal basilica built between 1400 and the end of the 16th c. is one of the most significant brick gothic churches in Bavaria, houses the **Moses Window** by Albrecht Dürer.

🏛 **St. Peter's Basilica**. northeast of the centre. Romanesque basilica from the 12th c. Sculpture portals and surrounding cemetery with several chapels are of interest.

- **Carmelite church**. Late gothic hall church with monks choir was redone in the baroque style in 1700 by Wolfgang Dientzenhofer.
- **Frauenbrünnl pilgrimage church** "Our Dear Lady", in the Stadtpark, west of centre. Baroque church built 1705-07.
- **Former ducal palace**. Irregularly constructed palace complex begun under Duke Albrecht I von Straubing-Holland in 1356.
- **Rathaus (Town hall)**. Three story main building with side wings and interior courtyard has its origin in the acquisition of a merchant's house in 1382. Numerous additions until the 19th c.
- **Stadtturm (City tower)**. Construction on the 68 m high medieval landmark, with four corner turrets around the central tower, was started in 1316 and continued until the end of the 16th c.
- **Spitaltor (Hospital gate)**. Late medieval gatehouse was completed in its current form in 1628.
- **Harness racing track**, Ejadonstr. 45, ✆ 3777. Races every 14 days on eastern Bavaria's largest harness racing track.
- **City and city-tower tours**, information at the tourism office.
- **Tiergarten (Zoo)**, Am Tiergarten 3, ✆ 21277, Open: Summer 8:30-18, Winter, 9-16. Eastern Bavaria's only zoo, with about 1,700 animals representing 200 species, and a unique aquarium for Danube aquatic life.
- **AQUAtherm**, Wittelsbacher Höhe 50/52, ✆ 864444, Open: Outdoor pool from mid-May to mid-Sept. Indoor pool mid-Sept. to mid-May.
- **Bund Naturschutz**, Albrechtsg. 3, ✆ 2512
- **Radhaus Lang**, Chamer Str. 36, ✆ 88353

46

☑ **Stadler**, Chamer Str. 47, ☎ 99200

☑ **Fahrzeughaus Simmerl**, Roseng. 45, ☎ 22539

The history of Straubing begins with a Celtic settlement called "Sorviodurum". It was followed by the Romans, who built several castra and a town. The Gäuboden museum displays numerous artefacts found in the region, of which the famous "Straubing Roman treasure" is especially noteworthy. Around 500 AD, a Bavarii clan, the "Strupinga" led by Strupo, moved into the settlement and gave it its current name. In 1218 Duke Ludwig der Kelheimer established the new city of Straubing. The city's oldest church is St. Peters, a prime example of Bavarian romanesque architecture. Its cemetery is also significant, with an extensive collection of gravestones representing every architectural style. In the 14th century the city tower was built on the market square, which is lined with impressive middle-class and patrician city houses. The Ursuline church was built by Bavaria's great masters of the baroque, the brothers Asam.

Straubing also hosts the Gäubodenfest around the 15th of August each year. It is Bavaria's second biggest beer and amusement festival, following Munich's famous Octoberfest, and includes a regional country fair.

Straubing to Deggendorf   40.1 km

Continue to the far end of the square, where it becomes the **Ludwigsplatz** ∼ turn left onto the street **Stadtgraben** ∼ cross the Danube and continue on the bicycle path along **Chamer Straße** ∼ after crossing the Old Danube on **Agnes Bernauer Bridge** turn right into **Ziererstraße** ∼ follow this

Deggendorf

street to the left along the dike ∼ go right on the quiet country road, which you follow to Reibersdorf.

Reibersdorf

Turn right and pass the church on the **Donaustraße** ∼ turn right as you leave the village and follow the path along the dike to Bogen ∼ **8** after the playing fields turn right onto the path along the Kinsach river and over the bridge to **Straubinger Straße** ∼ turn right across the railway line ∼ along **Bahnhofstraße** to Stadtplatz.

Bogen

Postal Code: 94327; Area code: 09422

🛈 **Tourist and Naturpark Info in the railway station**, Bahnhofstr. 26, ☎ 808855

🛈 **Kulturamt (culture office) Bogen**, Stadtpl. 56, ☎ 505109, www.bogen.de

🏛 **Local history museum on the Bogenberg**, ☎ 5786, Open: Wed, Sat 14-16, Sun/Hol 10-12 & 14-16. Farm tools and furniture, folk costumes and art from the 13th to 18th c.

🏛 **Motorcycle museum**, Untere Bergstr. 9, ☎ 1245, Open: by appointment.

🕍 **Maria Church on the Bogenberg**. Late gothic church finished in 1463, includes an unusual octagonal tower.

🚲 **e-bike verleih Bogen**, Straubinger Str. 4, ☎ 8593285

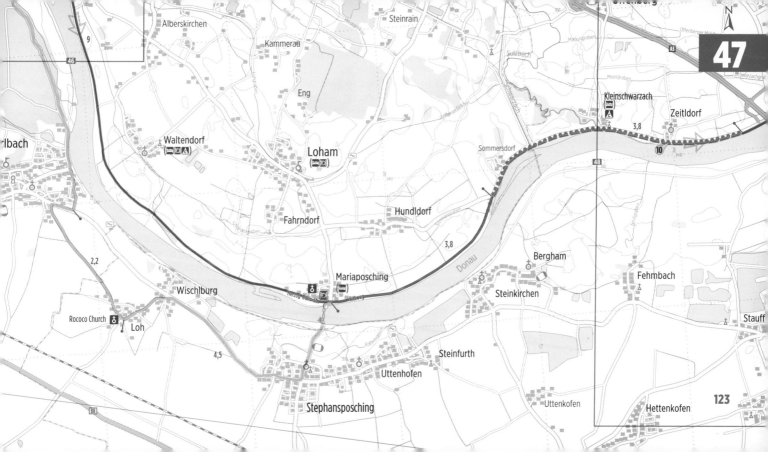

47

Alberskirchen

Kammerau

Steinrain

Sulzbach

9

Eng

Offenberger Mühle

A3

Schwarzachgr.

Moosgraben

46

Waltendorf

Loham

Kleinschwarzach

Zeitldorf

Ibach

3,8

Sommersdorf

10

48

Fahrndorf

Hundldorf

Donau

3,8

Bergham

Fehmbach

2,2

Wischlburg

Mariaposching

Herzog-Otto-Straße

Rittweg

Steinkirchen

Stauff

Rococo Church

Loh

4,5

Steinfurth

Uttenhofen

Hettenkofen

B8

Stephansposching

Uttenkofen

The history of Bogen can be traced back to the 8th century, when fishermen and traders started to settle at the mouth of the Bogenbach. In 1104 an event occurred which would make the Bogenberg famous. At the foot of the small mountain local residents found a statue of Mary which had presumably washed ashore from a sunken ship. Count Aswin installed the statue in a castle chapel, whereupon so many pilgrims began making their way to the village that he donated his palace to Benedictine monks of Oberalteichen. In 1679 Pater Balthasar Regler had the statue undressed for scientific purposes and discovered that the statue depicted a pregnant Mary. This prompted many pregnant women to begin making pilgrimages to the church to pray for comfort and healing. The pregnant Madonna seen in the church today is not the original. Historic reports show that during the Thirty Years War the Swedes tossed the statue off the rocky cliff above the Danube. But the statue got caught in the undergrowth and was later retrieved. Some believe that a stone Madonna that stands in a niche to the right from the choir may be the original 13th century statue.

The Stadtplatz (city square) in Bogen is dominated by two rows of attached buildings. Almost the entire western half of the market burned to the ground in 1719, and another fire destroyed a number of houses on the uphill-side of the market in 1835 and 1836. Construction of the royal Bavarian state court in Bogen sparked a new period of prosperity in Bogen. As the population grew, new schools and a hospital were built and in 1895 the railroad reached the town. In 1952 Bogen attained city status and has since developed into a modern small city.

Continue straight along **Deggendorfer Straße** out of Bogen ⁓ at the intersection, turn left into the small side street beside the main road, then continue on the bicycle path to Hofweinzier.

ALTERNATIVE In **Hofweinzier** you can switch to the other side of the Danube and proceed downstream via **Irlbach**, **Loh** and **Stephansposching**. This alternative is worthwhile if you wish to visit the Rococo church in Loh.

Continue on the bicycle path along the main road to Pfelling.

Pfelling

9 Take the underpass under the main road ⁓ turn left and follow the street past the houses ⁓ continue straight ahead across the small stream at the end of the village and follow the road along the Danube ⁓ keep right into the paved lane beside the river, which you follow all the way to the ferry landing in Mariaposching.

Mariaposching

EXCURSION In Mariaposching the ferry gives you another opportunity to visit the Rococo church in Loh-Wischlburg.

Continue along the river until the paved lane ends, where you can either continue on the gravel path along the top of the dike or ride with the traffic along the road until you reach **Zeitldorf 10** ⁓ continue on the path along the dike, which soon becomes a wide, paved path ⁓ you pass under a road bridge before reaching a parking area by a roundabout. To reach the centre of Metten turn left and ride straight through the roundabout.

Metten

Postal Code: 94526; Area code: 0991

🛈 **Tourism office**, Krankenhausstr. 22, ✆ 998050

Metten
Mettenbuch
Riedfeld
Benedictine Abbey
Aletsberg
Untermettenwald
Hirtzau
Schalterbach

Einkinn 510
B11
Thannberg
Deggendorf
Kleinfilling
Schleiberg
Gaisberg
390
Breitenberg
545
Leoprech

Offenberger Mühlbach
A3
arzach
Zeitldorf
Donau
3,8
10
Mettenufer
6
47
A3

Gailsberg
Simmling
Elmering
Old Town Hall
Holy Sepulchre
Rad-Info
Parish Church
Schiffsmeisterhaus "Info-Hafen"
Fischerdorf
Gailberg

Fehmbach
Natternberg
Elypso
Hauptstr.
Stauffendorf
3
49
Reinprechting

Rettenbach
Althofstr.
A92
Deggenau
125
Deggenauer Berg
410

11

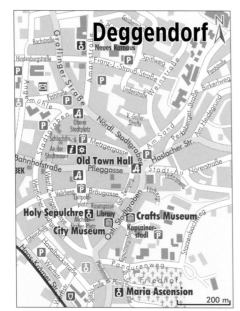

Deggendorf

Neues Rathaus

Old Town Hall

Holy Sepulchre *Library*

City Museum

Crafts Museum

Maria Ascension

200 m

Continue straight ahead along the river towards Deggendorf ~ the path comes to follow the dike ~ as you near the steel railway bridge turn left to the roundabout ~ ride straight ahead into the **Mettener Straße** ~ follow the bend of the street to the right ~ after passing under the railway bridge, turn right onto the bicycle path along **St.-Florian-Weg** ~ follow the bicycle path to the left parallel to the main road ~ continue straight through the underpass and **11** under the road bridge ~ follow the bicycle path along the main road, the **Neusiedler Straße**, becoming the **Hans-Krämer-Straße,** until you reach a large crossing with traffic lights by the church.

CENTRE To reach the historic centre of Deggendorf, turn left here and ride straight ahead through the old city gate.

Deggendorf

Postal Code: 94469; Area code: 0991

- **Tourist Information**, Oberer Stadtpl. 1, ✆ 2960535, www.deggendorf.de
- **Schiffmeisterhaus „Info Hafen"**, Schiffmeisterweg 10, ✆ 25040. Learn about water, environment and health from the exhibitions in this 400 year old "Shipmaster's House".
- **Passenger ship docks**, Deggendorf-Passau, May-Oct, Mon-Sat ✆ 0851/929292
- **City museum**, Östl. Stadtgraben 28, ✆ 2960555, Open: Tue-Sat 10-16, Sun 10-17. Presents the cultural, economic and social development of the city and the surrounding region.
- **Crafts museum (Handwerksmuseum)**, Maria-Ward-Pl. 1, ✆ 2960555, Open: Tue-Sat 10-16, Sun 10-17. Cultural history of local crafts.
- **Church of the Holy Sepulchre (Heilig-Grab-Kirche).** Dates to 1338. The baroque church tower was built 1722-27.
- **Maria Ascension (Mariä Himmelfahrt).** Construction started in 1655. Baroque high altar from the Eichstatt cathedral.
- **Altes Rathaus (Old town hall).** Built 1535 with distinctive gable and tower.
- **Bicycle boxes**, Neusiedler Straße, near the Stadthalle garage, ✆ 2960535
- **Zweirad Sport Salmannsberger**, Pferdemarkt 18, ✆ 30440
- **Fahrradshop**, Untere Vorstadt 10, ✆ 0176/26250190

Deggendorf's "pear-shaped" city limits reach way back to the middle-ages. Today a wide long market stretches down the middle of the city on two sides of the Old Rathaus with its imposing gothic tower. It is decorated with the crests of Bavaria and Deggendorf, with mythical animals and gargoyles, and with a medieval penal device, the "Schandkugeln" or "balls of dishonor", two stone balls connected by a length of chain. Heavy balls also figure in the Deggendorf dumpling legend, according to which the wife of one of the city's mayors was able to drive Bohemian invaders away with freshly-prepared dumplings.

In addition to the Rathaus, the two large parish churches, Maria Ascension and Church of the Holy Sepulchre, rank as the city's best known landmarks.

Deggendorf to Vilshofen an der Donau   31.6 km

Straight through the crossing in Deggendorf ~ follow the bicycle path along the busy **Hengersberger Straße** to **Deggenau** ~ follow the bicycle path on the right side of the road to the railway line ~ then along the right side of the railway line out of Deggenau ~ turn left at the T-intersection ~ you ride beside the freeway, then take the bridge over the freeway

50

to the Danube ~ continue beside the Danube past a bathing lake to the ferry landing in Niederalteich **12**. The centre of Niederalteich lies to the left.

Niederalteich

Postal Code: 94557; Area code: 09901

- 🛈 **Town office**, Guntherweg 3, ☎ 9353-0
- ⛴ **Bicycle ferry**, ☎ 935323, Operates: May-Oct, Mon-Fri 10-18, Sat, Sun/Hol 9-18.
- 🏛 **Aircraft Museum Gerhard Neumann**, Hengersberger Str. 5, ☎ 20270, Open: by arrangement
- ⛪ **Benedictine abbey Niederaltaich**, established in 731. The abbey church is one of the oldest gothic hall-churches, and was redone in baroque style in 1718.

Duke Odilo established the Niederaltaich Benedictine abbey in 731 AD. In the following centuries the abbey suffered major fires a total of 13 different times. From outside, the main gate recalls the abbey's gothic past while inside everything is done in the baroque style. It was here that the famous Bavarian tribal laws, the "Lex Baiuvariorum" were written down in the year 740.

FORK ▮ From Niederalteich you also have a signposted route on along the right bank of the Danube as far as Vilshofen.

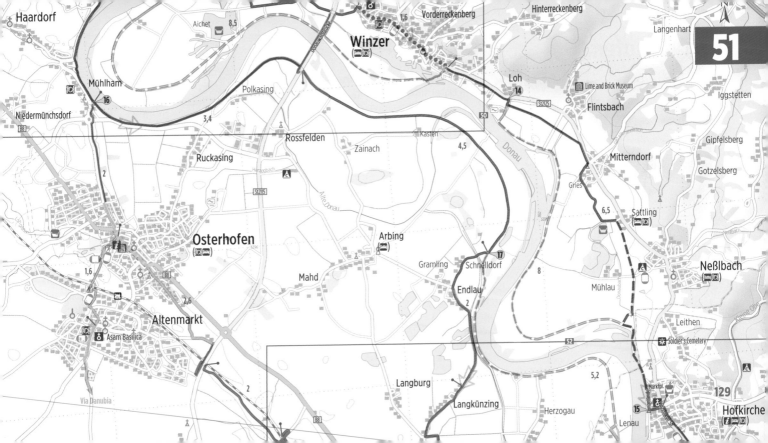

Vilshofen

Right bank to Vilshofen   **28 km**

After taking the ferry from Niederalteich, ride up the road to Thundorf.

Thundorf

Keep left by the church in Thundorf ～ then immediately turn left after crossing the ditch ～ follow the bicycle path along the dike out of Thundorf ～ in **Aicha** keep left and follow the path along the top of the dike to Haardorf.

Haardorf

Take the path to the left along the Danube ～ after the small bridge continue along the river bank past the houses of Mühlham ～ **16** at the end of the village you reach a small side street.

Mühlham

From here you have the option of visiting Osterhofen or taking advantage of the shorter alternative route to Künzing.

Alternative via Osterhofen   10 km

16 Turn right into the small side street and left on the main street ～ take the bicycle path straight through the roundabout and ride into the centre of Osterhofen, from where the excursion to the Asam Basilica in Altenmarkt is well signposted.

Osterhofen

Postal Code: 94486; Area code: 09932

🛈 **Tourist-Information**, Stadtpl. 13, ✆ 403115

🏛 **Local museum**, Stadtpl. 15, ✆ 1061, Open: Apr.-Oct., Sat, Sun 14-17.

🕍 **Asam Basilica**, Altenmarkt-Osterhofen. The St. Margareta cloister church was built in 1726 on the site of a medieval church.

From Osterhofen follow the signs for the **Osterhofen-Künzing** route to get you back to the main route in the centre of Künzing (Map 52).

Underway through the Gäuboden

The main route out of Mühlham continues along the dike ～ near **Polkasing** be sure to continue straight ahead along the dike ～ you reach a large road bridge, which you can use to connect with the route along the left bank, otherwise continue straight ahead under the bridge ～ follow the dike all the way to **Schnelldorf**, **17** where you follow the right bend in the road ～ continue past the houses of Schnelldorf to the T-intersection in **Gramling (Endlau)** ～ turn left and follow the street out of the village to Langkünzing.

Langkünzing

By the curve in the road at the end of the village turn left towards Künzing ～ follow the road to Künzing, where you keep right at the fork

after the bridge ～ ride to the T-intersection by the museum.

Künzing
Postal Code: 94550; Area code: 08549

- ⌂ **Museum Quintana**, Osterhofener Str. 2, ☎ 973112, Open: Tue-Sun 10-17. Here you can learn the settlement history spanning 7,000 years, from the early stone age over the Roman period to late antiquity.

Turn left and ride on the bicycle path along the main road to Pleinting ～ turn right after the first buildings ～ after passing the outdoor pool keep left onto the path past the tennis courts ～ continue along **Thanneter Straße** to the intersection.

Pleinting
Turn right and follow the main street **Hauptstraße** through Pleinting ～ **18** before the main road, turn right and ride through the railway underpass ～ keep left and follow the street parallel to the railway line out of Pleinting ～ keep left after passing under the bridge and continue beside the railway line into Vilshofen ～ at the end of the street take the pedestrian and bicycle path and turn left under the railway line ～ turn right, first exit, at the roundabout and ride to the next intersection by the historic

Vilshofen an der Donau

gate tower (Stadtturm) **19**. The historic centre of Vilshofen, centred on the **Stadtplatz**, lies straight ahead through the Stadtturm. Turn left to reach the bridge over the Danube and the main route to Passau on the left bank.

Vilshofen an der Donau
Postal Code: 94474; Area code: 08541

- ℹ **Tourist-Information**, Stadtpl. 27, ☎ 208112, www.vilshofen.de
- ⌂ **Gallery in the Stadtturm**, Open: Tue-Sun 14-17. Rotating exhibitions of contemporary artists.
- ⌂ **Town hall gallery**, Stadtpl. 27, ☎ 208-108
- ⌂ **Africa Museum**, in Schweiklberg Abbey, ☎ 209-0, Open: daily, 13:30-17.
- ⛪ **John the Baptist parish church**. 13th-14th c. gothic church was redone in the baroque style in 1803.

- ⛪ **St. Barbara church**. Late gothic church contains interesting Rococo altar from 1750. Situated in the cemetery.
- ⛪ **Maria-Hilf pilgrim church**. Domed church formed like an orthodox cross, built in 1692.
- ✦ **Rathaus (Town hall)**. Four-storey city hall built in the 16th century.
- ✦ **Art in public spaces**. Sculptures by regional artists on display in the historic centre.
- ☖ **Stadtturm (City tower)**. Landmark tower built 1642-47.
- ▢ **Outdoor Pool**
- ⚡ **Würdinger**, Kapuzinerstr. 107, ☎ 910710
- ⚡ **Charging station**, Am Bootshafen 1, ☎ 208112

Left bank to Vilshofen   *22 km*

In Niederalteich continue straight past the ferry landing on the paved lane along the dike ～ **13** after about 4 km turn left into the paved field road. Going straight takes you along the alternative route closer to the Danube.

Left again at the T-intersection ～ continue under the road bridge, which you can use to connect to the south bank route. To avoid Winzer, turn right after passing under the bridge, otherwise continue straight ahead ～ turn right on the main street, **Passauer Straße**, and ride through the town.

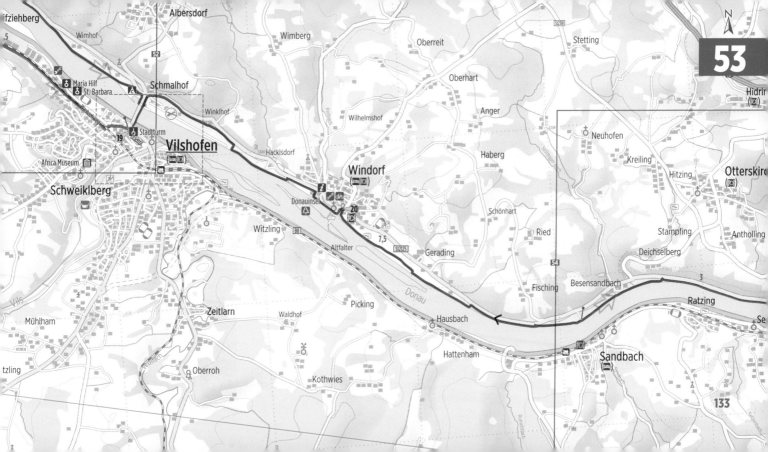

ifziehberg

,5

Albersdorf

Wimhof

Wimberg

Oberreit

Stetting

52

Schmalhof

Oberhart

Anger

Hidrir

Maria Hilf
St. Barbara

Winklhof

Wilhelmshof

Haberg

Neuhofen

Kreiling

Stadtturm

19

Vilshofen

Hacklsdorf

Hitzing

Otterskir

Africa Museum

Schweiklberg

Windorf

Schönhart

Stampfing

Antholling

Witzling

Donauinsel

20

Ried

54

Deichselberg

B8

7,5

Gerading

Fisching

Besensandbach

3

Altfalter

St2125

Ratzing

Mühlham

Zeitlarn

Waldhof

Picking

Donau

Hausbach

Se

Vils

Hattenham

Sandbach

tzling

Oberroh

Kothwies

133

Winzer

Postal Code: 94577; Area code: 09901

🛈 **Tourist Information**, Schwanenkirchener Str. 2, ✆ 93570

Ride along the main street out of the town, where you ride along the bicycle path until it ends in the hamlet of Loh.

Loh

14 Turn right opposite the houses of Loh ~ after 100 m turn left ~ ride straight along the paved field road to **Gries/Mitterndorf** ~ at the intersection by the houses in Gries turn right ~ keep left at the fork and ride past the houses ~ by the left bend, go straight out into the fields ~ follow the paved field road to a lake, where you turn left towards **Sattling** ~ stay right before the little bridge ~ follow the gravel field road, going straight at the next intersection ~ at the T-intersection by the next bridge keep right ~ turn left as you reach the dike and pump house by the Danube ~ follow the narrow path along the river into Hofkirchen, where you continue along the street **Donaulände**.

Hofkirchen

Postal Code: 94544; Area code: 08545

🛈 **Tourist-Information**, Rathausstr. 1, ✆ 97180, www.hofkirchen.de

---

🔵 **Maria Ascension parish church**, built in its current form in 1510, it is sometimes referred to as the Cathedral of the Danube valley.

🔵 **Kreuzberg chapel**, built in honor of Maria mother of god

✱ **Soldiers cemetery**, 2747 fallen soldiers from both world wars were buried here by the Volksbund Deutsche Kriegsgräberfürsorge. The memorial, north of Hofkirchen, is open to the public all year.

✱ **Apiculture (bee-keeping) trail**

🗆 **Outdoor pool**, heated, ✆ 313

Hofkirchen's existence can be traced back as far as the year 1005. It was granted market status in 1387 by Duke Albrecht the Younger. The city was an important landing station for the rafts and barge trains that plied the Danube until the mid-19th century. On October 18, 1745 Emperor Franz Stephan I spent the night in Hofkirchen as he traveled on his ship down the Danube after being crowned in Frankfurt.

15 Turn left into the street **Marktplatz** ~ then right on **Vilshofener Straße** ~ and take the bike path out of Hofkirchen ~ after the playing fields turn right towards Unterschöllnach ~ turn left before the wastewater treatment plant ~ turn right

---

after the bridge by **Unterschöllnach** ~ follow the paved lane, which takes you along the Danube to Hilgartsberg.

Hilgartsberg

🔒 **Hilgartsberg ruin**, possibly 12th c., rebuilt in the 17th c. Romanseque chapel with painted vaulting from the 16th c.

Continue on the wide bicycle path along the Danube until you reach the road bridge across the Danube ~ follow the bicycle path to the right past the marina ~ after passing under the bridge turn left up to the bicycle path along the main road.

▌From here you can take the bicycle path on the bridge across the Danube to visit Vilshofen.

Domplatz in Passau

Vilshofen an der Donau   **see page 132**

Vilshofen to Passau   *23.5 km*

Follow the bicycle path to Windorf ～ turn right as you reach the houses ～ follow the bicycle path along the river bank then left by the creek up to the main street **20**.

Windorf

Postal Code: 94575; Area code: 08541

🛈 Tourist-Information, Marktplatz, ☎ 962640

🚲 Bike & More, Marktpl. 12, ☎ 202570 or 0175/3664702

Turn right across the bridge and immediately right again ～ now simply follow the bicycle path along the river ～ you pass the ferry landing to Sandbach and shortly after the village of **Besensandbach** · **21** continue on the unpaved path along the river bank all the way to **Schalding** ～ turn right past the little marina and ride under the freeway bridge ～ after the underpass you cross the bridge over the river Gaißa ～ you now follow the bicycle path along the left side of the main road ～ continue along the street past **Donauhof** and **Wörth**, then back onto the bicycle path into **Maierhof** ～ take the underpass under the main road in Maierhof and continue on the bicycle

path along the right side of the road past the transformer station ~ turn right before the railway bridge ~ ride over the bridge by the **Kachlet locks** ~ **22** and continue over the barrage to the right bank of the Danube ~ turn left and follow the bicycle path along the river bank ~ under railway bridge and road bridge ~ at the T-intersection turn right and cross the main road ~ you now follow the bicycle path along the right side of **Regensburger Straße** all the way into the centre of Passau.

EXIT If you would like to get straight to the railway station, turn right into the **Bahnhofstraße** after the multi-storey car park.

Passau

Postal Code: 94032; Area code: 0851

🅸 **Tourist-Information**, Bahnhofstr. 28, ✆ 955980, www.passau.de

🅸 **Tourist-Information**, Rathauspl. 3, ✆ 955980

⚓ **Donauschifffahrt**, Wurm + Köck, Höllg. 26, ✆ 929292, Three-rivers tours daily from Mar.-Oct. in Passau and daily excursions to the Austrian Danube valley and Engelhartszell, Schlögen and Linz from Apr.-Oct.

🏛 **OberhausMuseum**, fortress Veste Oberhaus, ✆ 493350, Open: mid Mar.-mid Nov., Mon-Fri 9-17, Sat, Sun/Hol 10-18. History museum with exhibitions on city history, Böhmerwald museum,

Three rivers confluence, Passau

viewing tower. Shuttle bus from Apr.-Oct. departs from the Rathaus every 30 mins 10-17, Sat, Sun/Hol 10-8 every 30 mins.

🏛 **Glass Museum Passau**, in Hotel Wilder Mann, Rathausplatz, ✆ 35071, Open: daily 9-18. The 30,000 works of glass art provide an overview of European glass-making 1650-1950.

🏛 **Domschatz- u. Diözesanmuseum (Cathedral Museum)**, entrance through the cathedral. Open: May-Oct., Mon-Sat 10-16. History and artifacts from what was once the largest bishopric in the Holy Roman Empire.

🏛 **Kastell Boiotro Roman Museum**, Innstadt-Ledererg. 43, ✆ 34769. Open: Mar.-mid Nov., Tue-Sun 10-16. Exhibits include the excavated foundations of the Roman fort and archaeological discoveries from Passau and surrounding areas.

🏛 **Museum of Modern Art**, Altstadt, Bräug. 17, ✆ 3838790. Open: Tue-Sun 10-18. Alternating international exhibitions on 20th

century art presented in one of the most handsome old buildings in Passau.

🔯 **Veste Oberhaus**, Georgsberg. City fortress built 1219 by Passau's prince bishops. Today city property, houses museum.

🔯 **Veste Niederhaus**, at the mouth of the Ilz River. Probably built in the the 14th c. at the foot of the Oberhaus. In the 17th c. it served as a prison, later as a factory, today privately owned.

🔯 **St. Stephan cathedral**. The original cathedral was destroyed in 977. The current basilica was modelled on the church in Salzburg and finished in 1695. It is regarded the largest Italianate-baroque church north of the Alps, and also has the largest church organ in the world (17,974 pipes and 233 registers). Organ concerts early May-Oct., daily 12 o'clock except Sun /Hol.

🔯 **Niedernburg Monastery**, on the eastern tip of the city. Established in 740 and since 1836 used by the Sisters of Loretto. The church includes the grave of Giselle of Bavaria.

🎭 **Stadttheater (city theatre)**, Innbrücke. The former prince-bishop's opera house was built in 1783 and is Bavaria's only surviving early-classical theatre building.

✳ **Neue Residenz**, Residenzplatz. Built in the early 18th century according to the prince-bishop's taste, on the site of the early-medieval royal court. With a grand rococo stairs.

✳ **University and university church St. Nikola**, with 11th c. crypt.

✳ **Rathaus (town hall)**, Rathausplatz, Open: Easter-Oct daily 10-16. Grand baroque meeting hall in the town hall, with huge paintings

and 19th c. carillon in the tower: Mon–Sun 10:30, 14 & 19:25, Sat also 15:30.

⚫ **Three-rivers confluence**, of the Inn, Danube and Ilz rivers.

🚲 🔧 **Rent a Bike**, BIKEHAUS, railway station, ☎ 0151/12834224

🔧 🚲 **Fahrradklinik Passau**, Bräug. 10, ☎ 33411

🔧 🚲 **Fahrradladen Passau**, Wittg. 9, ☎ 72226

🔧 **Denk bike + outdoor**, Ludwigstr. 22, ☎ 31450

🔧 **Zweirad Seidel**, Spitalhofstr. 83, ☎ 57813

🔧 **Würdinger**, Regensburger Str. 22, ☎ 6346

🔧 **Zeller Zweirad**, Graneckerstr. 4, ☎ 56302

🚲 **Bicycle boxes**, Fahrrad Pensio Mandl, Bahnhofstr. 33, ☎ 34784

🚲 **Bicycle & baggage storage**, Donau-Schiffs-Reise-Centre, Untere Donaulände, ☎ 34262

🚲 **Bicycle boxes**, Obere Donaulände, key from Fahrradladen Passau, Wittg. 9, ☎ 72226

Passau, the three-rivers city, occupies a dramatic narrow peninsula formed by the Danube and Inn rivers. The third river, the Ilz, joins the Danube from the north near the city's eastern tip. Passau's history extends back to around 500 years BC. The original Celtic settlement was succeeded by the Romans around the time of Christ. In 460 AD St. Severinus, also known as the Apostle to Noricum, established a monastery here. In the 6th century, the Bavarii took control of what was the last Roman outpost on German soil. Batavis became Bazzava which finally became Passau. In 1161, the emperor withdrew from Passau and presented the Niedernburg Abbey to the high monastery of Passau, which governed the city until 1803. In 1568 Austrian nobles filled the prince-bishop's seat until Napoleon restored the city to Bavarian rule.

Passau's cathedral has gone through numerous incarnations. In the 13th century it was rebuilt as a gothic church. In 1407, Hans Krumenauer was instructed to build a completely new cathedral. It and large parts of the city were destroyed in a great fire in 1662. Because the city could not afford to build a new church at the time, the Italian architect Carlo Lurago added a baroque long-church to surviving elements of the gothic choir and transept. Today the church's interior is regarded as the largest baroque church space north of the Alps. The church also has five organs which can be played simultaneously from a single main console. It is considered the largest church organ in the world.

The city lies to the west of the Dreiflüsseeck, the point of the peninsula at which the three rivers join to form the Danube as it enters Austria. To the south lies the Innstadt, with the Mariahilf pilgrimage church. The Ilzstadt to the north is dominated by the lower Veste Niederhaus and the upper Veste Oberhaus fortress that offers excellent views on the panorama. Across from the cathedral one can find the "Passau Tölpel," or "idiot," jokingly considered the city's mascot. It is actually a fragment from a statue of St. Stephen, which fell from the cathedral's south tower and shattered during the fire of 1662.

PLANING In Passau you have the possibility of continuing your tour down the Danube, with detailed maps and information about the route from Passau all the way to the Black Sea available in the *bikeline* guides.

You have now reached the end of this cycling journey. We hope you had an interesting and enjoyable cycling holiday and we are pleased that you chose a *bikeline*-cycling guide to accompany you on your journey.

The *bikeline* team wishes you a safe and enjoyable return trip!

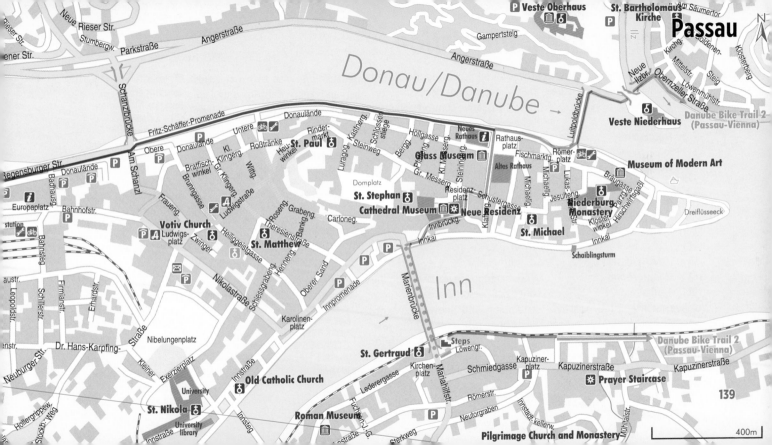

Passau

Donau/Danube →

Inn

Veste Oberhaus
St. Bartholomäus Kirche
Am Säumertor
Veste Niederhaus
Danube Bike Trail 2 (Passau-Vienna)
Museum of Modern Art
St. Paul
Glass Museum
Neues Rathaus
Rathaus-platz
Altes Rathaus
Fischmarktg.
Römer-platz
Niederburg Monastery
St. Stephan
Cathedral Museum
Domplatz
Residenz-platz
Neue Residenz
St. Michael
Votiv Church
Ludwigs-platz
St. Matthew
Schaiblingsturm
Dreiflüsseeck
Europaplatz
station
Bahnstr.
St. Gertraud
Steps
Löwengr.
Danube Bike Trail 2 (Passau-Vienna)
Old Catholic Church
Kirchen-platz
Kapuziner-platz
Prayer Staircase
Kapuzinerstraße
St. Nikola
University
University library
Roman Museum
Pilgrimage Church and Monastery

Neue Rieser Str.
Stumbergw.
Parkstraße
Angerstraße
Angerstraße
Gampertsteig
Rieser Str.
Wiener Str.
Neue Ilzbr.
Oberzeller Straße
Kirchg.
Goldenen-
Mittelstr.
Steig
Löwenmühlstr.
Obernzeller Straße
Regensburger Str.
Schanzlbrücke
Fritz-Schäffer-Promenade
Donaulände
Untere Donaulände
Obere Donaulände
Donaulände
Luitpoldbrücke
Badhausg.
Bahnhofstr.
Am Schanzl
Kl. Klingerg.
Heu-winkel
Brattfisch-winkel
Gr. Klingerg.
Roßtränke
Rinder-markt
Höllgasse
Schlosser-stiege
Steinweg
Luragog.
Kastnerg.
Bergg.
Kl. Messerg.
Gr. Messerg.
Steining.
Schustergasse
Michaelig.
Lukasg.
Jesuiteng.
Braug.
Kloster-winkel
Hischwirtsgäßl
Partok.
Wittg.
Ludwigstraße
Brunngasse
Frauengasse
Rosenghasse
Grabeng.
Carloneg.
Theresiensthraße
Heiliggeistgasse
Henneng.
Schlessgrabeng.
Nikolastraße
Zwinger
Innbrückg.
Innkai
Klarg.
Innkai
Oberer Sand
Innpromenade
Marienbrücke
Karolinen-platz
Nibelungenplatz
Exerzierplatz
Kleiner Exerzierplatz
Dr. Hans-Karpfing-
Neuburger Str.
Leopoldstr.
Schillerstr.
Firmianstr.
Erhardtstr.
Straße
Innstraße
Innsteg
Ledererg.
Fuchsg.
Römerstr.
Mariahilfstr.
Schmiedgasse
Neutorgraben
Innstadt-kellerw.
Mühldstr.
Römerstr.
Sterkweg
Hollerzipfelweg
Stockö-weg

139

400m

Overnight Accommodation

The following list includes accommodation in the following categories:

H   Hotel
Hg   Hotel garni
Gh   Inn
P   Pension
Pz   Private room
BB   Bed and Breakfast
Fw   Apartment (selected)
Bh   Farm
Hh   Hay hotel
🏠   Youth Hostel
⚠   Campground
⚠   Tent site

We have not attempted to list every possible place where visitors can spend the night, and listings should not be construed as any kind of recommendation. The Roman number (I-VII) after the telephone number indicates price range.

These fall into six categories, listed below, and do not necessarily reflect the relative comfort and quality available. Please be aware that prices can vary according to room type, season or during trade fairs.

I   less than € 15
II   € 15 to € 23
III   € 23 to € 30
IV   € 30 to € 35
V   € 35 to € 50
VI   € 50- € 70
VII   over € 70

These categories are based on the price per person in a double room equipped with shower or bath, with breakfast, unless otherwise indicated. Rooms with bath or shower in the hall are indicated with the symbol ⚐. The symbol ◎ indicates ADFC-certified BettBike accommodation.

Because we wish to expand this list and keep it up-to-date, we welcome any comments, additions or corrections you may have. There is no charge for a listing.

Donaueschingen
Postal code: 78166; Area code: 0771
🛈 Tourist-Information, Karlstr. 58, ✆ 857221
Gh Jägerhaus, Buchberg 37, ✆ 7346, IV ◎
P Ziegelhof, Dürrheimer Str. 65, ✆ 3373, III
H Parkside Hotel Concorde, Dürrheimer Str. 82,
✆ 83630, V
H Wyndham Garden Donaueschingen, Hagelrainstr. 17,
✆ 8986440, VI-VII
H Waldblick, Am Hinteren Berg 7, ✆ 832520, V
H Grüner Baum, Fr.-Ebert-Str. 59, ✆ 80910, V ◎
H Linde, Karlstr. 18, ✆ 83180, V-VI ◎
H Zum Hirschen, Herdstr. 5, ✆ 898558-0, V ◎
Gh Adler, Bregstr. 3, ✆ 2401, III
P Baarblick, Peter-Maier-Str. 3, Hubertshofen,
✆ 07705/97003, III
Pz Schuhmann, Holzsteigweg 31, ✆ 5999, II
Pz Rothweiler, Schubertstr. 1, ✆ 4479, III
Pz Schmid, Schwalbenweg 16, ✆ 13277, II ⚐

Pfohren
Postal code: 78166; Area code: 0771

⚠ Riedsee-Camping, Am Riedsee 11, ✆ 5511

Neudingen
Postal code: 78166; Area code: 0771
Gh Linde, ✆ 61853, III

Gutmadingen
Postal code: 78187; Area code: 07704
Pz Bensel, Alemannenstr. 20, ✆ 6972, II
Pz Draxler, Schulstr. 17, ✆ 484, II
Pz Schmid, Alemannenstr. 26, ✆ 6747, III
Pz Stahnke, Waldstr. 17, ✆ 6865, II

Geisingen
Postal code: 78187; Area code: 07704
🛈 Rathaus, Hauptstr. 36, ✆ 807-0
P Gästehaus arena geisingen, Mühltorg. 1, ✆ 9233980,
II
Gh Hecht, Hauptstr. 41, ✆ 281, V
P Jasmin, Schlossstr. 29, ✆ 6097, II
Pz Kurz, Nikolausstr. 10, ✆ 919697, III
Pz Frey, Karl-Wacker-Str. 1, ✆ 6953, II
Pz Mini-Villa Kunterbunt, Hauptstr. 11, ✆ 0171/4968762,
II
Pz Rudigier, Am Kalkofen 4, ✆ 6742, III
Pz Stoffler, Schillerstr. 8, ✆ 6198, III
Pz Zöllner, Droste-Hülshoff-Str. 16, ✆ 923600, III

Kirchen-Hausen
Postal code: 78187; Area code: 07704

H Sternen, Ringstr. 1-4, ✆ 8039, V
Gh Mond, Aitrachtalstr. 17, ✆ 80090, III
Pz Gotthardt/Limbach, Gauertstr. 4, ✆ 9239981
Pz Jurischitz, Münsterg. 2, ✆ 0162/4544991, II
Pz Weber, Auf Hochstetten 19, ✆ 1342, II
Pz Wittenberg, Im Ried 1, ✆ 8620, II

Immendingen
Postal code: 78194; Area code: 07462
ℹ️ Tourist-Information, Schlosspl. 2 ✆ 24228
Gh Waldhorn, Zimmern, Hornensteigstr. 1, ✆ 1284, III
P Panda, Hindenburgstr. 9, ✆ 923438, III
Pz Böhler, Kastanienweg 10, ✆ 1226, II

Möhringen
Postal code: 78532; Area code: 07462
ℹ️ Tourist-Info, Hermann-Leiber-Str. 4, ✆ 948220
Gh Zum Löwen, Mittlere G. 4, ✆ 6277, V
Gh Hecht, Hechtpl., ✆ 6287, III-IV
P Donaupension, Esslinger Str. 12, ✆ 269191, III
P B&B, Schwarzwaldstr. 18, ✆ 269316, VI
P La Cascina, Schwarzwaldstr. 33, ✆ 269287
Pz Waibel, Gihrsteinstr. 8, ✆ 6321, II
Naturfreundehaus Donauversickerung, Konzenberg-
    str. 1, ✆ 91323, II 🍴

Vorstadt
Area code: 07461
P Classica,Grünebergstr. 31, ✆ 4284, II

Tuttlingen
Postal code: 78532; Area code: 07461
ℹ️ Tourismus Tuttlingen, Rathausstr. 1, ✆ 99340

Gh Rössle, Honbergstr. 8, ✆ 2913, IV 🍴
H Landhotel Hühnerhof, Äußerer Talhof 2, ✆ 96550 🍴
H Schlack, Bahnhofstr. 59, ✆ 9440, V-VI
H Stadt Tuttlingen, Donaustr. 30, ✆ 9300, VI
H Ritter, Königstr. 12, ✆ 966330, IV-V
H Légère Hotel Tuttlingen, Königstr. 25, ✆ 96160 🍴
Hg Rosengarten, Königstr. 17, ✆ 96270, V
Pz Bayrak, Liptinger Str. 115, ✆ 9087552, III
Pz Becker, Albrecht-Dürer-Str. 69, ✆ 9635811, III
🏕️ Zeltplatz im Umläufle, ✆ 99340

Wurmlingen
Postal code: 78573; Area code: 07461
H Traube, Untere Hauptstr. 43, ✆ 9380
Gh Zum Löwen, Karlstr. 4, ✆ 93300, V 🍴

Nendingen
Postal code: 78532; Area code: 07461
P Da Nino, Industriestr. 22/1, ✆ 162273, IV
Gh zur Rose, Rosenstr. 14, ✆ 3635, III

Stetten
Postal code: 78570; Area code: 07463
Gh Zum Lamm, Rathausstr. 6, ✆ 393, III

Mühlheim a. d. Donau
Postal code: 78570; Area code: 07463
ℹ️ Verkehrsamt, Vorderes Schloss, ✆ 8903
Gh Krone, Tuttlinger Str. 1, ✆ 7043, III-IV
P Gästehaus Theresia, Schloss 8, ✆ 5070, III 🍴
Gh Hirsch, Hauptstr. 6, ✆ 498,II-III
Gh Zur Linde, Bergstr. 16, ✆ 7855, II-III
Pz Kunz, Hauptstr. 28, ✆ 7725
Pz Beutel, Siedlungstr. 2, ✆ 995784
Pz Korb, Zeppelinstr. 19, ✆ 7917
Pz Leibinger, Schönenbergstr. 23, ✆ 7399

Fridingen
Postal code: 78567; Area code: 07463
ℹ️ Verkehrsamt, ✆ 8370
H Sonne, Bahnhofstr. 22, ✆ 99440, III-V 🍴
H Landhaus Donautal, Bergsteig 1, ✆ 469, V
H Knopfmacher, Knopfmacherfelsen 1, ✆ 1057, IV
Gh Löwen, Mittlere Gasse 3, ✆ 9942-0, IV-V
Gh Jägerhaus, Im Donautal, ✆ 07466/254, V
Gh Vesperstube Ziegelhütte, ✆ 8996, IV
Pz Reiser, Martin-Kempter-Str. 4, ✆ 7804
Pz Sattler, Am Wendelstein 5, ✆ 1325, III 🍴
Pz Perazic, Litschenberg 1, ✆ 7634, III

Beuron
Postal code: 88631; Area code: 07466
ℹ️ Tourist-Information, Hausen, Kirchstr. 18
    ✆ 07579/92100
H Haus Maria Trost, Edith-Stein-Weg 1, ✆ 483, V
H Pelikan, Abteistr. 12, ✆ 406, V
P Gregoiushaus, Wolterstr. 9, ✆ 284428, III
Pz Haus Schönwalder, Donaustr. 5, ✆ 1294, II-III
Bh Der Talhof, Talhof 2, ✆ 07579/933143 🍴
🏰 Burg Wildenstein, 88637 Leibertingen, ✆ 411

Hausen im Tal
Postal code: 88631; Area code: 07579
ℹ️ Tourist-Information, Kirchstr. 18, ✆ 9210-0
Gh Murmeltier, Kirchstr. 9, ✆ 93126, I-II
Gh Steinhaus, Schwenninger Str. 2, ✆ 9339789, IV
Gh Bahnhof, Bahnhof 2, ✆ 565, III
Pz Küchenhoff, Panoramastr. 13, ✆ 397, II
Pz Wagenburg, Panoramastr. 10, ✆ 2722, II
Pz Haus Maria, Gartenstr. 12, ✆ 1455, II
🏕️ Camping Wagenburg, ✆ 559

Neidingen
Postal code: 88631; Area code: 07579
Gh Mühle, Neidinger Str. 47, ✆ 523, II

Thiergarten
Postal code: 88631; Area code: 07570
Gh Berghaus, Waldstr. 1, ✆ 951562, III-V 🍴
Gh Neumühle, Neumühle 1, ✆ 9590, III-IV
Gh Gutshof Käppeler, Hofstr. 22, ✆ 951910, III
Pz Ferienhaus Wolf, Hofstr. 2, ✆ 1443, II

Gutenstein

Postal code: 72488; Area code: 07570

 H Backpackers-Hotel, Burgfeldenstr. 37-1, ☎ 07575/1221, III

Gh Zum Bahnhof, Langenharterstr. 9, ☎ 279, III

Pz Bürkle, Schiffgarten 3, ☎ 1318, III-IV

Pz Seifried, Burgfeldenstr. 30, ☎ 452, III

▲ Youth tent site Aisnau, Burgfeldenstr. 27, ☎ 487

Dietfurt

Postal code: 72514; Area code: 07571

🅸 Mayor's office Inzigkofen, ☎ 73070

Pz Dietfurter Mühle, Burgstr. 10, ☎ 51715

Vilsingen

Postal code: 72514; Area code: 07571

🅸 Mayor's office Inzigkofen, ☎ 73070

Gh Zoller, Dorfstr. 33, ☎ 51089, III

Fw Donau, Dr.-Josef-Vögte-Str. 7, ☎ 51669, V

Inzigkofen

Postal code: 72514; Area code: 07571

🅸 Mayor's office Inzigkofen, Ziegelweg 2, ☎ 73070

P Kreuz, Rathausstr. 15, ☎ 51812, III

Pz Haus Armella, Weidenweg 2, ☎ 51696, I

Pz Riester, Kirchstr. 8, ☎ 14124

Fw Villa Donautal,Reischacherstr. 8, ☎ 682718, II

Sigmaringen

Postal code: 72488; Area code: 07571

🅸 Tourist Information, Leopoldpl. 4, ☎ 106224

H Fürstenhof, Zeppelinstr. 14, ☎ 72060, V

Hg Jägerhof, Wentelstr. 4, ☎ 744990, V 🌊

Gh Traube, Fürst-Wilhelm-Str. 19, ☎ 64510, V 🌊

Gh Donau, Donaustr. 1, ☎ 4612, III-IV

Gh Alter Fritz, Zimmerackerstr. 5, ☎ 12059, III

P Pfefferle, Leopoldstr. 22, ☎ 2448, IV-V 🌊

P Schmautz, Im Muckentäle 33, ☎ 51554, IV-V

P Eichamt, Donaustr. 15, ☎ 0171/6811802, V

Pz Leichtle, Bussenstr. 23, ☎ 5568, III

🏠 Hohenzollern-Jugendherberge Sigmaringen, Hohenzollernstr. 31, ☎ 13277, II-III 🌊

▲ Camping Sigmaringen, Georg-Zimmerer-Str. 6, ☎ 50411

Sigmaringendorf

Postal code: 72517; Area code: 07571

🅸 Mayor's office, ☎ 73050

Gh Unterm Regenbogen, Oberdorf 8/1, ☎ 683892, V

H Hirsch, Lauchertbühl 9, ☎ 72060, III

H Beim Rinderwirt, Hauptstr. 17, ☎ 13743 🌊

Pz Schmitt-Speh, Laizer Öschle 39, ☎ 12647, III

Scheer

Postal code: 72516; Area code: 07572

🅸 Mayor's office, ☎ 76160

H Donaublick, Bahnhofstr. 21-28, ☎ 76380, V 🌊

Pz Biehler, Leonhardsweg 10, ☎ 1238, II

Pz Eisele, Am Grabenweg 4, ☎ 2198, II

Ennetach

Postal code: 88512; Area code: 07572

P Dorfstuben, Ablachweg 6, ☎ 712995, IV 🌊

Pz Knoch, Keltenweg 4, ☎ 8556, II

Pz Kirchenbauer, Keltenweg 2, ☎ 5288, II

Pz Herla, Keltenweg 3, ☎ 8824, II

Pz Hertes, Gartenstr. 58, ☎ 8401, II

Mengen

Postal code: 88512; Area code: 07572

🅸 Tourist-Info Mengen, Bürgerbüro Mengen, Hauptstr. 90, ☎ 6070

H Baier, Hauptstr. 10, ☎ 76210, III-IV

H Rebstock, Hauptstr. 93, ☎ 76680, III-V

H Zum Fliegenwirt, Flugpl. 34, ☎ 760340

Pz Schenk, Weidenstr. 15, ☎ 78409, II 🍴

Blochingen

Postal code: 88512; Area code: 07572

Pz Kuchelmeister, Egelseeweg 4, ☎ 2513

Fw Haus Renate, Lattenbachstr. 8, ☎ 2603

Herbertingen

Postal code: 88518; Area code: 07586

🅸 Local Council, Holzg. 6, ☎ 92080

Gh Engel, Bahnhofstr. 1, ☎ 92110, I-II

Gh Sonne, Sonnenstr. 10, ☎ 370, I

Hundersingen

Postal code: 88518; Area code: 07586

Gh. Adler, Ortsstr. 1, ☎ 378, IV

Ertingen

Postal code: 88521; Area code: 07371

🅸 Mayor's office, Dürmentingerstr. 14, ☎ 5080

Gh Buck, Edith-Paiters-Gässle 11a, ☎ 44152, II 🌊

Neufra

Postal code: 88499; Area code: 07371

H Kleinstes Schlosshotel, Schlossberg 12, ☎ 5700, V 🌊

Altheim

Postal code: 88499; Area code: 07371

Gh Donautal, Donaustr. 75, ☎ 93702-0, V 🌊

Pz Rettich, Lindenweg 6, ☎ 3963, oder 0177 8990677

H Kloster Heiligkreuztal, Am Münster 7, ☎ 931230, teilw. 🍴 🌊

Pz Gentner, Sandgrubenweg 1, ☎ 965144, II

Riedlingen

Postal code: 88499; Area code: 07371

🅸 Information in the Rathaus, Marktpl. 1, ☎ 1830

H Charisma Hotel Brücke, Hindenburgstr. 4, ☎ 12266, IV

Gh Hirsch, Lange Str. 17, ☎ 7365, II-III

Gh Rosengarten, Gammertinger Str. 25, ☎ 7336, IV-V

Pz Landhaus am Vogelberg, Josef-Christian-Str. 39,

✆ 10377, III
Pz Herz-Stüble, Berliner Str. 37, ✆ 8907, II
Pz Scheffold, Josef-Christian-Str. 34, ✆ 3537, II
🔺 Weiss, Vöhringerhof, ✆ 12574
🔺 Tent site for cyclists, by the Tennishalle, ✆ 13620

Grüningen
Postal code: 88499; Area code: 07371
Gh Adler, Adlerberg 10, ✆ 93410, III

Unlingen
(2 km von Daugendorf nach Südosten)
Postal code: 88527; Area code: 07371
Gh Sonne, Hauptstr. 7, ✆ 8574, IV
Gh Am Eck, Kirchg. 12, ✆ 8242, II–III; 🖭
Haus der Gesundheit, Klostermauer 11, ✆ 7890
🔺 Tent site by the Haus d. Gesundheit

Daugendorf
Postal code: 88499; Area code: 07371
ℹ Information in the Rathaus, Riedlingen, ✆ 1830

Baach
Postal code: 88529; Area code: 07373
P Auchter, Talweg 12, ✆ 1422, III 🖭

Zwiefaltendorf
Postal code: 88499; Area code: 07373
Gh Zum Rössle, Von-Speth-Str. 19, ✆ 643, II–III

Zwiefalten
Postal code: 88529; 07373
Touristinformation, in the town hall, Marktpl. 3,
✆ 20520
Fw Aachtalblick, Bussenblick 32, ✆ 915299

🔺 Youth tent site at the Höhenfreibad, ✆ 20520

Rechtenstein
Postal code: 89611; Area code: 07375
ℹ Mayor's office, Braunselweg 2, ✆ 244
Gh Zur Brücke, Karl-Weiß-Str. 1, ✆ 257, II
Bahnhofsgaststätte, Bahnhofstr. 9, ✆ 315, I
🔺 Tent site Mittenhausen, ✆ 361

Obermarchtal
Postal code: 89611; Area code: 07375
Gh Berghofstüble, Reutlingendorferstr. 5, ✆ 266, III–IV 🖭
P Bildungshaus Kloster Obermarchtal, Klosteranlage2/1, ✆ 95050, III–V

Munderkingen
Postal code: 89597; Area code: 07393
ℹ Town hall, Marktstr. 1, ✆ 5980
P Cafe Blank/Adler Brasserie, Martinstr. 17, ✆ 91424, II–III
H Café Knebel, Donaustr. 21, ✆ 1314, III–IV 🖭
Gh Rose, Donaustr. 2, ✆ 1726, II 🖭
Pz Nöbel, Gerhard-Hauptmann-Weg 12, ✆ 919283, II
🔺 Tent site Bodenösch, ✆ 0160/8709619

Rottenacker
Postal code: 89616; Area code: 07393
ℹ Mayor's office, Bühlstr. 7, ✆ 95040
Gh Teufel's Dorfwirtschaft, Bogenstr. 19, ✆ 95480
🔺 Tent site Badesee „Heppenäcker", ✆ 01716825016

Dettingen
Postal code: 89584; Area code: 07391

Gh Knupfer, Rottenacker Str. 15, ✆ 2488, III 🖭

Berg
Postal code: 89584; Area code: 07391
H Rose, Graf-Konrad-Str. 5, ✆ 70830, IV–V 🖭

Ehingen
Postal code: 89584; Area code: 07391
ℹ Tourist-Info, Marktpl. 1, ✆ 503-207 or -216
H Ehinger Rose, Hauptstr. 10, ✆ 2737, V 🖭
H Ehinger Hof, Lindenstr. 28, ✆ 77070, V
Gh Sonne, Sonneng. 5, ✆ 6885, III
H Ochsen, Schulg. 3, ✆ 770530, VI 🖭
H Adler, Hauptstr. 116, ✆ 70660, VI
H Bestwestern Bierkulturhotel Schwanen, Schwaneng. 18-20, ✆ 770850 🖭
H Linde, Lindenstr. 51, ✆ 58050, VI
Gh Hirsch, Kirchen, ✆ 07393/9501-0, V
Gh Lamm, Am Kussenberg 18, ✆ 1764, IV
P & Fw Wittmaack, Weberg. 34, ✆ 7819066 o. 0171 9820148
Gh Rössle, Hauptstr. 171, ✆ 53465, IV
Hg Panorama, Karpfenweg 7, ✆ 77460, V
Fw Weber, Veilchenweg 4, ✆ 53620, II

Allmendingen
Postal code: 89604; Area code: 07391
ℹ Village office, Hauptstr. 15, ✆ 70150
P Schloss-Mühle, Schwenkstr. 6, ✆ 2002
H Adler, Hauptstr. 23, ✆ 52068
Gh Sportheim, Am Sportplatz

Griesingen
Postal code: 89608; Area code: 07391
ℹ Council office, Alte Landstraße, ✆ 8748
Gh Adler, Alte Landstr. 12, ✆ 8373, III

Blaubeuren
Postal code: 89143; Area code: 07344
ℹ Tourism office, Achg. 7, ✆ 921025 or 96690
P Ohm, Gerberg. 21, ✆ 910100, V
H Ochsen, Marktstr. 4, ✆ 969890, V–VI
H Adler, Karlstr. 8, ✆ 91770, V 🖭
H Löwen, Markpl. 1, ✆ 92805-0, V
Gh Blautopf, Blautopfstr. 4, ✆ 95246-6, IV 🗡
Fw Blaubeuren, Weilerstr. 19, ✆ 9247095
🏠 Jugendherberge, Auf dem Rucken 69, ✆ 6444

Herrlingen
Postal code: 89134; Area code: 07304
ℹ Bürgermeisteramt, Marktpl. 2, ✆ 8020
Gh Lindenmeir, Bahnhofstr. 9, ✆ 921328, III–IV

Blaustein
Postal code: 89134; Area code: 07304
ℹ Town office, Marktpl. 2, ✆ 8020
H Kalte Herberge, Ulmer Str. 30, ✆ 96190, V

Nasgenstadt
Postal code: 89584; Area code: 07391
Hg Panorama, Karpfenweg 7, ✆ 77460, IV–V

Öpfingen
Postal code: 89614; Area code: 07391
ℹ Mayor's office, Schlosshofstr. 10, ✆ 7084-0
Gh Ochsen, Darreng. 42, ✆ 6129 or 53150, III

Ersingen
Postal code: 89155; Area code: 07305
- Local administration, Mittelstr. 11/1, ✆ 9262880
- Gasthaus Hirsch & Campingplatz, Rißtisser St. 4, ✆ 4160
- Campground at the bathing lake, information DLRG, ✆ 7460

Erbach
Postal code: 89155; Area code: 07305
- City office, Erlenbachstr. 50, ✆ 96760
- Gh Schwabenpfanne, Donaustetter Str. 21/1, ✆ 24444, IV
- H Zur Linde, Bahnhofstr. 8, ✆ 931100, IV ◉
- H Kögel, Ehinger Str. 44, ✆ 8021, IV-V
- P Adler, Erbacher Str. 1, ✆ 6309, IV
- P Steinle, Kirchenberg 12, Donaurieden, ✆ 5216, III ◉

Donaustetten
Postal code: 89079; Area code: 07305
- P „Bed & Breakfast", Eichbühlstr. 68, ✆ 4610, IV
- Gh Zum Kreuz, Alb-Donau-Str. 17, ✆ 7160, III ◉

Gögglingen
Postal code: 89079; Area code: 07305
- Hg Am Zehntstadl, Bertholdstr. 17, ✆ 9613-0, V ◉
- Gh Zum Ritter, Bertholdstr. 8, ✆ 95654-0, III

Wiblingen
Postal code: 89079; Area code: 0731
- H Löwen, Hauptstr. 6, ✆ 880312-0, VII

Ulm
Postal code: 89073; Area code: 0731

144

- Tourist Information, Münsterpl. 50, ✆ 1612830
- H Anker, Rabeng. 2, ✆ 63297, IV-V ◉
- H Am Rathaus, Kroneng. 8-10, ✆ 968490, V-VI
- H Akzent Hotel Roter Löwe, Ulmer G. 8, ✆ 14089-0, VI
- H Bäumle, Kohlg. 6, ✆ 62287, V
- H Comfor, Frauenstr. 51, ✆ 96490, VI
- H Ibis Budget, Neutorstr. 16, ✆ 17662720, IV
- H Goldenes Rad, Neue Str. 65, ✆ 800184, V-VI
- H InterCity, Bahnhofpl. 1, ✆ 96550, VI-VII
- H Ibis, Neutorstr. 12, ✆ 96470, V
- H Maritim, Basteistr. 40, ✆ 9230, VII
- H Schiefes Haus, Schwörhausg. 6, ✆ 967930, VII
- H Schwarzer Adler, Frauenstr. 20, ✆ 6025000, III
- H Stern, Sterng. 17, ✆ 15520, V-VI
- H Blaubeurer Tor, Blaubeurer Str. 19, ✆ 93460, VI
- H Ulmer Stuben, Zinglerstr. 11, ✆ 962200, V
- Hg B&B Hotel Ulm, Ehinger Str. 9-11, ✆ 176330, IV
- Hg Münster Hotel, Münsterpl. 14, ✆ 64162, IV
- Hg Lehrertal, Lehrer-Tal-Weg 3, ✆ 954000, ◉
- Hg Neuthor, Neuer Graben 17, ✆ 9752790, V-VI
- P Rösch, Schwörhausg. 18, ✆ 65718, III
- Jugendherberge Ulm, Grimmelfingerweg 45, ✆ 384455 ◉

Grimmelfingen
- H O Sole Mio, Eisenbahnstr. 47, ✆ 382575, V
- H Hotel Adler, Kirchstr. 12, ✆ 938080, V
- H Hotel Hirsch, Schultheißenstr. 9, ✆ 937930, V

Neu-Ulm
Postal code: 89231; Area code: 0731
- Tourist Information Ulm, Münsterpl. 50, ✆ 1612830

- H Brauhaus Barfüßer, Paulstr. 4, ✆ 97448-0, V
- H City-Hotel, Ludwigstr. 27, ✆ 97452-0, V
- H Meinl, Marbacher Str. 4, ✆ 70520, VI-VII ◉
- H Golden Tulip Parkhotel, Silcherstr. 40, ✆ 80110, VI-VII
- H Orange Hotel, Dieselstr. 4, ✆ 37846570, V
- Hg Donau-Hotel, Augsburger Str. 34, ✆ 97690, V
- Gh Rose, Kasernstr. 42a, ✆ 77803, II
- P Hotel Schiff, Hermann-Köhl-Str. 18a, ✆ 0175/6138656, II-III
- P Mitte 24, Kasernstr. 24, ✆ 0178/5661593, III-IV
- BB Brickstone Hostel, Schützenstr. 42, ✆ 7082559, II-III

Pfuhl-Offenhausen
Postal code: 89233; Area code: 0731
- H Sonnenkeller, Leipheimer Str. 97, ✆ 71770, V
- Hg Kreuzäcker, Augsburger Str. 196, ✆ 9742325, V
- Hg Schmid, Hauptstr. 67, ✆ 979900, V
- Gh Engel, Augsburger Str. 192, ✆ 9747100, III-IV

Thalfingen
Postal code: 89275; Area code: 0731
- Town office, Pfarrg. 2, ✆ 20660
- H Austüble, Austr. 26, ✆ 263135, III

Oberelchingen
Postal code: 89275; Area code: 07308
- Gh Krone, Klostersteig 38, ✆ 2586, IV

Unterelchingen
Postal code: 89275; Area code: 0731
- Gh Adler, Finkenweg 1, ✆ 2805, II-IV
- Gh Zahn, Hauptstr. 35, ✆ 3007, IV

Riedheim
Postal code: 89340; Area code: 08221
- Hh, Fw & ⚠ Schwarzfelder Hof, Schwarzfelder Weg 3, ✆ 72628

Leipheim
Postal code: 89340; Area code: 08221
- Tourist-Information Günzburg-Leipheim, 89312 Günzburg, ✆ 200444
- HH Zur Post, Bahnhofstr. 6, ✆ 2770, IV ◉
- Hg Leipheimer Hof, Schlosshaldenring 68, ✆ 71560, IV
- Gh Hirschbräu, Ulmer Str. 1, ✆ 71411, ◉
- Gh Bären, Günzburger Str. 15, ✆ 72047, III
- Gh Waldvogel, Grüner Weg 1, ✆ 27970, IV
- Pz Hawlitschek, Schillerstr. 13, ✆ 200733

Günzburg
Postal code: 89312; Area code: 08221
- Tourist-Information Günzburg-Leipheim, Schlosspl. 1, ✆ 200444
- H Zettler, Ichenhauser Str. 26A, ✆ 36480, VI
- H Arcadia, Am Hofgarten, ✆ 3510, VI
- H Hirsch, Marktpl. 18, ✆ 5610, IV
- H Goldener Löwe, Ichenhauser Str. 62, ✆ 36680, V
- Hg Bettina, Augsburger Str. 68, ✆ 36220, V-VI
- Hg Römer, Ulmer Str. 26, ✆ 367380 ◉
- Gh Rose, Augsburger Str. 23, ✆ 2068211, V ◉
- Gh Zur Münz, Marktpl. 25, ✆ 9167494, V-VI
- Pz Kindermann, Roseng. 14, ✆ 33716, II
- Pz Geduld, Auf der Bleiche 5, ✆ 33673, II
- Pz 8-Mädchenhaus, Ichenhauser Str. 53, ✆ 1719, II ✂
- Fw Ferienwohnungen am Weiher, Am Weiher 8,

☎ 963341 ⊚
Fw Erika, Am Weiher 4, ☎ 21743 ⊚
🏠 Naturfreundehaus Am Birket, Schmiedlweg 2, ☎ 2788299, II
⛺ Tent site by the Naturfreundehaus, Schmiedlweg 2, Anmeldung bei Fr. Pleier, ☎ 2788299

Offingen
Postal code: 89362; Area code: 08224
ℹ Council office, Marktstr. 19, ☎ 96970
Gh Krone, Hauptstr. 34, ☎ 1739
Pz Wiedenmann, Herrenwörtherstr. 11, ☎ 2370, II

Gundelfingen a. d. Donau
Postal code: 89423; Area code: 09073
ℹ Culture office in the Rathaus, Prof.-Bamann-Str. 22, ☎ 999118

Gh Zur Schützen, Bahnhofst. 24, ☎ 9974787, V
Gh Stadion, Stadionstr. 1, ☎ 2406 ⊚
Gh Zur Sonne, Hauptstr. 56, ☎ 7334, IV ⊚
Gh Zur Alten Kanzlei, Am Wehrgang 9, ☎ 969159, IV ⊚
Gh Zum Stiftsgarten; Lauinger Str. 25, ☎ 920713, II
Gh Wünsch, Äußere Offinger Str. 2a, ☎ 508, III
P Kneipe am See, Offinger Str. 2, ☎ 508, III

Gundelfingen-Echenbrunn
Postal code: 89423; Area code: 09073
Gh Sonne, Lauinger Str. 52, ☎ 958640, IV

Faimingen
Postal code: 89415; Area code: 09072
Pz Weimer, Magnus-Scheller-Str. 3, ☎ 920989

Lauingen
Postal code: 89415; Area code: 09072
ℹ City office, Herzog-Georg-Str. 17, ☎ 9980
H Kastanienhof, Bahnhofstr. 4, ☎ 96030, IV-V
H Genießerhotel Lodner, Imhofstr. 7, ☎ 95890, V ⊚
H Drei Mohren, Imhofstr. 6, ☎ 95610, IV
Gh Rose, Herzog-Georg-Str. 4, ☎ 921841
Gh Kannen Keller, Dillinger Str. 26, ☎ 7070
Gh Schimmel, Herzog-Georg-Str. 12, ☎ 2450, I o. Frühst.

Dillingen
Postal code: 89407; Area code: 09071
ℹ Tourist information, Königstr. 37, ☎ 54208
H Zur Donau, Donaustr. 7, ☎ 58520, III
H Convikt, Konviktstr. 9, ☎ 79130, V-VI
H Dillinger Hof, Rudolf-Diesel-Str. 8, ☎ 58740, V-VI ⊚
Hg Trumm, Donauwörther Str. 62, ☎ 3072, IV

Gh Zur Traube, Königstr. 46, ☎ 726060, IV-V
P Gästehaus der Franziskanerinnen, Kard.-v.-Waldburg-Str. 2, ☎ 79280 (Gruppen), III
🏠 Eichwaldstuben, Georg-Schmid-Ring 45, ☎ 728445 (jugenherbergsähnlich), III
⛺ Donau-Camping, Georg-Schmid-Ring 45, ☎ 728445

Hausen
Gh Sonne, Wittislinger Str. 9, ☎ 2201, III
Pz Kling, Frauenalstr. 6, ☎ 1780, II (o. Frühstück)

Steinheim
Postal code: 89407; Area code: 09074
Pz Burggraf, Tannenbühl 1, ☎ 3553, III
Fw Müller, Dillinger Str. 18a, ☎ 5229, II

Höchstädt an der Donau
Postal code: 89420; Area code: 09074
ℹ Tourism office, Herzog-Philipp-Ludwig-Str. 10, ☎ 4412
Gh Glocke, Friedrich-v.-Teck-Str. 12, ☎ 957885, IV-V
H Berg, Dillinger Str. 17, ☎ 958990, III-V
Pz Maier, An der Bleiche 23a, ☎ 6691, I-II ⊚
Pz Thomas, An der Bleiche 26, ☎ 0172/6057531, II
Pz Geierhos, Bachg. 28, ☎ 2191, II
⛺ Camping Roth, Mörslingen, ☎ 4024

Deisenhofen (nordwestl. v. Höchstädt)
Gh Schildenberger, Steinheimer Str. 3, ☎ 4933, II

Sonderheim
Postal code: 89420; Area code: 09074

Gh Zur Alten Donau, Hauptstr. 4, ☎ 3220, III-IV
Gh Heigl, Paulstr. 1, ☎ 1066, II
Pz Linder, Höchstädter Str. 4, ☎ 761, II

Blindheim
Postal code: 89434; Area code: 09074
P Breisachmühle, Nebelbachstr. 15, ☎ 6166, III
Pz Konle, Schlossstr. 2, ☎ 91027, III

Wolperstetten
Pz Baur, Wolperstetten 4, ☎ 407, II

Gremheim
Postal code: 89443; Area code: 09070
Pz Sailer, St.-Georg Str.1, ☎ 629, II

Schwenningen
Postal code: 89443; Area code: 09070
H Schloss Kalteneck, Kirchstr. 26, ☎ 90994-0, IV
Gh Zum Lamm, Bundesstr. 7, ☎ 258, II-III

Buttenwiesen
Postal code: 86647; Area code: 08274

Lauterbach
Gh Bräustüble, Bahnhofstr. 16, ☎ 1666, II

Pfaffenhofen
P Haus Kapfer, Am Brühl 9, ☎ 1391,II

Tapfheim
Postal code: 86660; Area code: 09070
Gh Bäldleschwaige, Bäldleschwaige 1, ☎ 217, II

Erlingshofen
Postal code: 86660; Area code: 09070
Gh Zur Grenz, ☎ 456, II
Karthäuserklause, ☎ 302, II-III

Zusum

Postal code: 86609; Area code: 0906

P Gerstmeier, St.-Sebastian-Str. 5, ✆ 4513, II

Asbach-Bäumenheim

Postal code: 86663; Area code: 0906

H Assos, Römerstr. 41, ✆ 9315, III

Donauwörth-Wörnitzstein

Postal code: 86609; Area code: 0906

Gh Zum Schidbaur, Zollernweg 2, ✆ 70622-0, V

Donauwörth

Postal code: 86609; Area code: 0906

🛈 City Tourist Information, Rathausg. 1, ✆ 789151

H Promenade, Spindeltal 3, ✆ 70593440, V

H Donau, Augsburger Str. 6, ✆ 7006042, V-VI

H Donauwörther Hof, Teutonenweg 16, ✆ 5950, III-IV

H Drei Kronen, Bahnhofstr. 25 ✆ 706170, IV-VI

H Parkhotel, Sternschanzenstr. 1, ✆ 706510, VI-VII

H Goldener Greifen, Pflegstr. 15, ✆ 705826-0, IV-VI

H Viktoria, Artur-Proeller-Str. 4, ✆ 7057080, V

H Posthotel Traube, Kapellstr. 14-16, ✆ 706440, V

Hg Pension Parkstadt, Andreas-Mayr-Str.11, ✆ 4039, V

Gh Goldener Hirsch, Reichsstr. 44, ✆ 3124, IV-V

Gh Landgasthof Schmidbaur, Zollernweg 2, ✆ 706220, III-V

Gh Pension Buena Vista, Hindenburgstr. 29, ✆ 9998825, III

Gh Zum Deutschmeister, Hochbruckerstr. 2, ✆ 8095, IV-V

Gh Feuerle-Ragusa, Heilig-Kreuz-Str. 4, ✆ 3733, III

Gh Zum Bären, Gartenstr. 15, ✆ 9800850, III

P Dietenhauser, Rainer-Str. 50, ✆ 9800677, III-IV

P Gerstmeier, St.-Sebastian-Str. 5, Zusum, ✆ 4513, III

P Graf, Zirgesheimer Str. 5, ✆ 5117, II-III

Pz Degginger, Posthof 2a, ✆ 28418, II-III

Pz Heidi, Sonnenstr. 5, ✆ 09090/4344

Pz Linder, Ölg. 2, ✆ 0175/2778972, II-III

BB Donauwörth, Schützenring 8, ✆ 7057871, III

🏠 Jugendherberge Donauwörth, Stadtteil Berg, Goethestr. 10, ✆ 5158 🌐

🏕 Tent site at the Kanu-Club, An der Westspange, ✆ 22605

Parkstadt (mit Anstieg)

Hg Parkstadt, Andreas-Mayr-Str. 11, ✆ 4039, IV-V

Gh Zum Deutschmeister, Hochbruckerstr. 2, ✆ 8095, IV-V

Zirgesheim

Postal code: 86609; Area code: 0906

Gh Mayer, Schenkensteiner Str. 9, ✆ 706690, IV

Pz Mebes, Lederstätterstr. 6, ✆ 22035, II

Pz Leberle, Schießerhof 1, ✆ 1323, I-III

Altisheim

Postal code: 86687; Area code: 09097

Bh, Wirth, Hopfenweg 1, ✆ 263, II

Pz Steidle, ✆ 1212, I

Marxheim

Postal code: 86688; Area code: 09097

Gh Bruckwirtschaft Marxheim, Flößstr. 8, ✆ 920435

P Schütz, Pfalzstr. 10, ✆ 1047, II

P Weigl, Schweinspoint, ✆ 288

🏕 bei Gh Sonne, ✆ 239

Bertholdsheim

Postal code: 86643; Area code: 08434

🛈 Visitors information Neuburg, Neuburg an der Donau, ✆ 08431/55-240 or 241

Gh Schloßgaststätte, Am Schossberg 2, ✆ 552, II

Pz Seefried, Finkenstr. 14, ✆ 1806, II 🌐

Pz Roßkopf, Lerchenstr. 7, ✆ 650, II

Hatzenhofen

Postal code: 86643; Area code: 08434

P Hager, Graspointstr. 19, II

Stepperg

Postal code: 86643; Area code: 08434

Gh Kimmerling, Poststr. 5, ✆ 9163, III

Bittenbrunn

Postal code: 86633; Area code: 08431

H Kirchbaur-Hof, Monheimer Str. 119, ✆ 619980, V

Laisacker:

P Jagdschlößl, Gietlhausener Str. 43, ✆ 2700, II

P Dollinger, Gietlhausener Str. 42, ✆ 7234, II

P Memmelhof, Brunnenstr. 13, ✆ 2529, III

Neuburg an der Donau

Postal code: 86633; Area code: 08431

🛈 Tourist-Information, Ottheinrichplatz A 118, ✆ 55-240/-241

H Am Fluss, Ingolstädter Str. 2, ✆ 6768-0, VI

H Neuwirt, Färberstr. 88, ✆ 2078, III-V 🌐

Gh Blaue Traube, Amalienstr. 49, ✆ 8392, II-III

H Garni, Schrannenpl. C 153 1/2 ✆ 67210, III

H Kieferlbräu, Eybstr. 239, ✆ 67340, IV

Hg Am Fluss, Ingolstädter Str. 2, ✆ 67680, V-VI

Hg Die Spindel, Mühlenweg 2a, ✆ 49423, IV

P Reissner, Mühlenweg 25 1/2, ✆ 44067, III

Pz Kerner, Ostermannstr. 55, ✆ 2398, II

🏠 JUST Jugendübernachtung, Adolf-Kolping-Str. 298 1/2, ✆ 57285

🏕 Youth tent site Schwaighölzl, Grünauer Str., ✆ 57285

🏕 Public camping facility of the Donauruderklubs (300 m downstream from the Danube bridge), Oskar-Wittmann-Str. 5, ✆ 9474

Weichering

Postal code: 86706; Area code: 08454

Gh Vogelsang, Bahnhofstr. 24, ✆ 91260, V

Pz B&M, Bahnhofstr. 26, ✆ 8503, III

Ingolstadt

Postal code: 85049; Area code: 0841

🛈 Tourist-Information, Rathauspl. 2, ✆ 3053030

Hg Ebner, 85053, Manchinger Str. 78, ✆ 966500, V

Hg Bauer, 85053, Hölzlstr. 2, ✆ 67086, V

H Adler, Theresienstr. 22, ✆ 35107, VI

H Ammerland, 85055, Ziegeleistr. 64, ✆ 953450, V-VII

H Zum Anker, Tränktorstr. 1, ✆ 30050, V

H Altstadthotel, Gymnsaiumstr. 9, ✆ 8869-0, V-VII

H ARA, 85055, Schollstr. 10a, ✆ 95430, V-VII

H ARA Comfort, 85055, Theodor-Heuss-Str. 30, ✆ 95550, V-VII

H Bavaria, 85055, Feldkirchener Str. 67, ✆ 95340, V

H Bayerischer Hof, Münzbergstr. 12, ✆ 934060, V
H Domizil, 85055, Feldkirchner Str. 69, ✆ 954530, V-VI
H Donauhotel, 85051, Münchener Str. 10, ✆ 965150, V
H enso, Bei der Arena 1, ✆ 885590, VI-VII
H Hecht, 85055, Regensburger Str. 77, ✆ 58507, V
H Pfeffermühle, 85053, Manchinger Str. 68, ✆ 965020, V
H NH Ambassador, 85055, Goethestr. 153, ✆ 5030, VI-VII
H Schumann-Stuben, 85057, Schumannstr. 21, ✆ 81435, III
Gh Gambrinus, F.-Ebert-Str. 32, ✆ 56160, V 🍴
Gh Kleines Brauhaus, Levelingstr. 86, ✆ 81077, V
Gh Zur Linde, Geibelstr. 6, ✆ 8816400, IV-V
P Eisinger, 85051, Dorfstr. 17a, ✆ 973660, IV
P Torkel-Stube, Feselenstr. 52, ✆ 69665, IV
BB Hotel Ingolstadt, Schollstr. 4, ✆ 95560, IV
⛺ Azur, Am Auwaldsee, ✆ 9611616, Open: all year
🏠 Friedhofstr. 4 1/2 ✆ 3051280, ◉

Großmehring
Postal code: 85098; Area code: 08407
ℹ Rathaus, Marienpl. 7, ✆ 9294-0
Gh Delagera, Nibelungenstr. 51, ✆ 373, III
Gh Zur alten Schule, Regensburger Str. 30, ✆ 1430, III

Vohburg
Postal code: 85088; Area code: 08457
ℹ City office, Ulrich-Steinberger-Pl. 12/13, ✆ 92920
Gh Stöttner-Bräu, Donaustr. 9, ✆ 1219, II-III
P Lohr, Auertorstr. 31, ✆ 7602 or 415, II
Gh Zur Sonne, Donaustr. 33, ✆ 1216, II
Gh Vis a Vis, Donaustr. 7, ✆ 930104

Pz Dankmeier, Max-Bogner-Str. 8, ✆ 930112
⛺ Tent site, Donaulände

Menning
Gh Unterer Wirt, Ingolstädter Str. 17, ✆ 929412, II
⛺ Private tent site by the „Unteren Wirt", ✆ 929412

Irsching
Pz Laube, Germanenstr. 11, ✆ 1096

Dünzing
Postal code: 85088; Area code: 08457
Pz Amberger, Dorfstr. 34a, ✆ 2951
Pz Wolfsteiner, Am Ölberg 1, ✆ 1751

Wackerstein
Postal code: 85104; Area code: 08403
Pz Anna Kreis, Vohburger Str. 82, ✆ 731

Neustadt a. d. Donau
Postal code: 93333; Area code: 09445
ℹ Tourist Information, Bad Gögging, ✆ 0800/46344464 or 95750
Gh Gigl, Herzog-Ludwig-Str. 6, ✆ 9670, IV ◉
Gh Amtmann, Herzog-Ludwig-Str. 9, ✆ 2872, II
⛺ Campingplatz Felbermühle, ✆ 516

Bad Gögging
Postal code: 93333; Area code: 09445
ℹ Tourist Information, Heiligenstädter Str. 5, ✆ 0800/46344464 or 95750
H Zur Post, ✆ 95470, V
H Centurio-Felicitas, Am Brunnenforum 6, ✆ 97220, IV-V ◉
H Zur Sonne, Trajanstr. 3-5, ✆ 95470, III

H Minerva-Dian, Zur Limestherme 3, ✆ 880, ◉
H Monarch, Kaiser-Augustus-Str. 36, ✆ 980 ◉
H Marc Aurel, Heiligenstädter-Str. 36, ✆ 9580, VI
H Eisvogel, An der Abens 20, ✆ 9690, V
H Kurhotel Kaiser Trajan, Römerstr. 8, ✆ 9660 ◉
P Amann, Römerstr. 10, ✆ 97130, II
P Haus Brigitte, Am Stocket 12, ✆ 95520, II
P Eichschmid, Römerstr. 4, ✆ 991920, II
P Antonius, Zur Limestherme 8, ✆ 95580, II
P Erika, Römerstr. 13, ✆ 573, I
P Holzapfel, Trajanstr. 14, ✆ 95510, II
P Kolb, Neustädter-Str. 22, ✆ 1720, II
P Marcus, Am Stocket 19, ✆ 95610, II
P Martinus, Heiligenstädterstr. 23, ✆ 95620, II
P Reger, Heiligenstädterstr. 11, ✆ 200040, II
P Schwaiger, Schulstr. 7, ✆ 95670, II

Eining
Postal code: 93333; Area code: 09445
Gh Abusina Stubn, ✆ 8359, I
Pz Treitinger, ✆ 7880

Weltenburg
Postal code: 93309; Area code: 09441
ℹ siehe Kelheim
P Ferienhof Weltenburg, Alte Dorfstr. 1, ✆ 3550, III-IV
P Probst, Auf der Weiß 10, ✆ 9546, III
P Köglmaier, Am Keltenwall 4, ✆ 7103, III

Kelheim
Postal code: 93309; Area code: 09441
ℹ Tourist-Information, Rathaus, ✆ 701234
Gh Frischeisen, Regensburger Str. 69, ✆ 50490, III

P Carlbauer, Schlossbuckel 4, ✆ 50380, IV
H Altstadthotel Wittelsbacher Hof, Donaustr. 22-26, ✆ 17705-0, VI
H Altes Kloster, Klosterstr. 5, ✆ 50150, V
Gh Weißes Lamm, Ludwigstr. 12, ✆ 20090, V
Gh Stockhammer, Am oberen Zweck 2, ✆ 70040, V
Gh Cafe am Donautor, Donaustr. 19, ✆ 50250, IV
Gh Sperger, Regensburger Str. 190, ✆ 3420, III
Gh Berzl, Hafnerg. 2, ✆ 1425, IV
P Dietz, Ludwigspl. 11, ✆ 2444, IV
Pz Sedlmayer, Traubenweg 29, ✆ 294157, III
P Zum Schwan, Fischerg. 30, ✆ 29298, IV
P Piccolo-Piccolo, Meisenstr. 2, ✆ 642844, II-III
Pz Ingerl, Robert von Welzstr. 6, ✆ 2486, II 🍴
Pz Riepl, Kiesweg 11, ✆ 3003, II
🏠 Jugendherberge Kelheim-Ihrlerstein, 93346 Ihrlerstein, Kornblumenweg 1, ✆ 3309
⛺ Camping am Bauernhof, Alfons Poschenrieder, Herrnsaaler Ring 26, ✆ 9607

Kelheimwinzer
Postal code: 93309; Area code: 09441
Gh Winzer, Dorfring 23, ✆ 5899, III
Pz Glaser, Pfarrer-Plass-Weg 7, ✆ 9158, II 🍴
Pz Weinzierl, Dorfring 17, ✆ 4947, III
Pz Stark, Dorfring 11, ✆ 9313, III
Pz Rengstl, Winzerberg 11, ✆ 4117, II

Kapfelberg
⛺ Campingplatz Kapfelberg, Bootsweg 3, ✆ 09405/ 5335

Poikam

🏕 Campingplatz Poikam, Kanalstr. 22, 93077Bad Abbach/Poikam, ✆ 09405/4431

Lengfeld

Postal code: 93077; Area code: 09405

Gh Schreiner, Teugner Str. 11, ✆ 1717, III

Bad Abbach

Postal code: 93077; Area code: 09405

ℹ Resort offices, Kaiser-Karl-V.-Allee 5, ✆ 95990

H Elisabeth, Ratsdienerweg 4-8, ✆ 95090, V
H Park-Cafe Reichl, Kaiser-Karl-V.-Allee 28, ✆ 2171, V
H Parkresidenz, Kochstr. 18-20, ✆ 95000, V ◙
H Cafe Rathaus, Kaiser-Karl-V.-Allee 6, ✆ 5009060, V
H Zur Post, Am Markt 21, ✆ 95360, IV
H Kötterl, Am Markt 12, ✆ 2339, III
Gh Wastlwirt, Gerhart-Hauptmann-Str. 25, ✆ 4569, III
P Toscana, Bahnhofstr. 14, ✆ 95440, IV
P Marion, Kochstr. 21, ✆ 5009060, II I ◙
P Isabella, Frauenbrünnlstr. 23, ✆ 1757, III
P Berghofer, Kochstr. 14, ✆ 2278, III
P Claudia, Frauenbrünnlstr. 24, ✆ 1031, III
P Geitner, Frauenbrünnlstr. 12a, ✆ 3188, III
P Brunner, Peisingerstr. 1, ✆ 3724, III
P Huber, Kochstr. 3, ✆ 941268, III
P Am Burgberg, Schulbruck 2a, ✆ 918389, III
P Hermann, Kaiser-Karl-V.-Allee 54, ✆ 2423, II

Matting

Postal code: 93080; Area code: 09405

Gh Fänderl, Matting, Wirtsweg 2, ✆ 2105
Fw Gebhard, Matting, Hanselbergweg 4, ✆ 3118

Pentling

Postal code: 93080; Area code: 09405

H Zur Walba, Unterirading 1, ✆ 2102 ◙

Regensburg

Postal code: 93047-93059; Area code: 0941

ℹ Tourist-Information, Altes Rathaus, Rathauspl. 4, ✆ 5074410, www.regensburg.de

H Münchner Hof, 93047, Tändlerg. 9, ✆ 58440, V-VI ◙
H Bischofshof Braustuben, 93049, Dechbettener Str. 50, ✆ 2082170, VI
Gh Spitalgarten, 93059, St.-Katharinen-Pl. 1, ✆ 84774, III
H Blauer Turm, 93047, Tändlerg. 14, ✆ 58440, VI-VII ◙
H Central Regensburg CityCentre, 93047, Margaretenstr. 18, ✆ 298484-0, VII
H Dicker Mann – Hotel Zum Blauen Krebs, 93047, Krebsg. 6, ✆ 57370, VI
H L'Ostello Altstadthotel, 93047, Schäffnerstr. 20, ✆ 63087490, VI
H Abotel, Donaustaufer Str. 70, ✆ 64090585, V ◙
H STAR INN Hotel, 93047, Bahnhofstr. 22, ✆ 5693-0, V
H Best Western Premier, 93051, Ziegetsdorfer Str. 111, 46393-0, VI
H ZAR Hotel Vitalis, 93051, Dr.-Gessler-Str. 29, ✆ 29859-0, V
H Wiendl, 93053, Universitätsstr. 9, ✆ 92027-0, V
H Stadthotel Regensburg, 93051, Gutenbergstr. 17, ✆ 992557-55, IV
H Orphée Landhaus – Andreasstadel, 93059, Andreasstr. 26, ✆ 5960-2300, VI-VII

H Jakob, Jakobstr. 14, ✆ 6009290, VII
H Lux, 93059, Stadtamhof 24, ✆ 85724, V
H Altstadthotel Arch, 93047, Haidpl. 4, ✆ 58660, VI-VII
H Courtyard by Marriott, 93059, Frankenstr. 28, ✆ 81010, V-VII
H DB Gästehaus, 93049, Klosterackerweg 1, ✆ 500312, IV
H Goliath am Dom, 93047, Goliathstr. 10, ✆ 2000-900, VII
H Orphée Großes Haus, 93047, Untere Bach. 8, ✆ 596020, V-VII
H Ibis Budget Regensburg, 93055 Junkersstr. 1, ✆ 789541, III
H Held, 93055 Irl 11, ✆ 094019420, VI
H Regensburger Hof, 93055, Adolf-Schmetzer-Str. 33, ✆ 60030, IV-V ◙
H St. Georg, 93051, Karl-Stieler-Str. 8. ✆ 91090, V
H Bischofshof am Dom, 93047, Krauterermarkt 3, ✆ 58460, VII
H Atrium im Park, 93059, Im Gewerbepark D90, ✆ 40280, V-VI
H Apollo Hotel, 93051, Neuprüll 17, ✆ 91050, V
H Mercure Hotel Regensburg, 93053, Grunewaldstr. 16, ✆ 78820, VI
H Das Götzfried Kultur & SPA Hotel, 93057, Wutzlhofen 1, ✆ 69610, VI-VII ◙
H Orphee „Kleines Haus", 93047, WahlenStr. 1, ✆ 596020, V-VI
H Eurostars Park Hotel Maximilian, 93047, Maximilianstr. 28, ✆ 56850, VI-VII

H Sorat Insel-Hotel, 93059, Müllerstr. 7, ✆ 81040, VI
H Avia, 93059, Frankenstr. 1-3, ✆ 40980, V-VI
H Ibis City, 93053, Furtmayrstr. 1, ✆ 78040, IV
H Kaiserhof am Dom, 93047, Kramg. 10-12, ✆ 585350, V-VI
H Roter Hahn, 93047, Rote-Hahnen-G. 10, ✆ 595090, VI
H Am Peterstor, 93047, Fröhl.-Türken-Str. 12, ✆ 54545, III
H Hansa Apart-Hotel, 93051, Friedenstr. 7, ✆ 99290, VII
H Altstadthotel Am Pach, 93047, Untere Bachg. 9, ✆ 29861-0, VI
H Goldenes Kreuz, 93047, Haidpl. 7, ✆ 55812, VI
H Achat Plaza Herzog am Dom, 93047, Dompl. 3, ✆ 584000, VII
H Altstadt-Engel, 93047, Gesandtenstr. 12, ✆ 280746-00, VI
H Castle Hotel, 93047, St. Petersweg 3, ✆ 58612707, VI
H Elements Hotel, 93047, Alter Kornmarkt 3, ✆ 38198600, VI
H Hottentotten Inn, Auweg 1a, ✆ 69099999, V
H Dock 1, Alte Straubinger Str. 7, ✆ 6009090, V
H Kolpinghaus, 93047, Adolph-Kolpingstr. 1, ✆ 595000, V ◙
Hg Zum Fröhlichen Türken, 93047, Fröhliche-Türken-Str. 11, ✆ 53651, V ◙
Gh Spitalgarten, 93059, St.-Katharinen-Pl. 1, ✆ 84774, III
Gh Parzefall, Obertraublinger Str. 54, ✆ 71459, VI
Gh Parklounge, Salzburgerg. 1, ✆ 3070412
Gh Dechbettener Hof, 93051, Dechbetten 11, ✆ 35283, V

P Holzgarten, Holzgartenstr. 77, ✆ 78036550, IV

P Katholische Akademie, 93047, Osteng. 27, ✆ 5696-30, V

Pz Zimmer in Regensburg, Weißgerbergraben 8/Rehgäßch. 5, ✆ 7957893 📷

🏠 Brook Lane Hostel, Obere Bachg. 21, ✆ 6900966

🏠 Jugendherberge, 93059, Wöhrdstr. 60, ✆ 57402 📷

⛺ Azur-Camping, 93049, Weinweg 40, ✆ 270025

Tegernheim
Postal code: 93105; Area code: 09403

H von Heyden, Von-Heyden-Str. 26, ✆ 954499400

H Mc Dreams, Von-Heyden-Str. 12, ✆ 954110

Gh Götzfried, Donaustr. 13, ✆961665, III

Fw Bavarian Cottage, Ringstr. 14, ✆ 967767

Donaustauf
Postal code: 93093, Area code: 09403

🛈 Touristinfo Donaustauf, Maxstr. 24, ✆ 9552929

H Forsters, Maxstr. 43, ✆ 9100 📷

Gh Hammermühle, Thiergartenstr. 1, ✆ 96840, V 📷

Pz Kastenmeier, Ludwigstr. 30, ✆ 1014, II

Sarching
Postal code: 93092, Area code: 09403

Gh Geser, Kirchpl. 4, ✆ 952900, IV

Gh Karl-Wirt, Obere Dorfstr. 17, ✆ 9529-20, III

P Pension am Donaubogen, Obere Dorfstr. 28, ✆ 2467, V

Demling
Postal code: 93090; Area code: 09403

Pz Kaiser, Rosenstr. 6, ✆ 8506

Pz Wagner, Alleestr. 14, 2250

Bach a. d. Donau
Postal code: 93090; Area code: 09403

P Held, Hauptstr. 44, ✆ 1881, III

P Weinstube Heitzer, Obere Bachg. 9, ✆ 954832, III

Pz Gmeinwieser, Obere Bachg. 7, ✆ 2529

Wiesent
Postal code: 93109; Area code: 09482

P Rösch, Regensburger Str. 10, ✆ 3706, III

Fw Stadler, Ettersdorfer Str. 9, ✆ 3536

Wörth
Postal code: 93086; Area code: 09482

🛈 Tourism office, Rathauspl. 1, ✆ 94030

P Bayerisches Gästehaus, Osserstr. 5, ✆ 2805, II

H Rosenhof, Straubinger Str. 21, ✆ 2080, III-IV

Gh Butz, Kirchpl. 3, ✆ 9510, III

Gh Geier, Josef-Feller-Str. 1, ✆ 2250, II-III 📷

Pz Fuchs, Hungersdorfer Str. 2, ✆ 2856, II

Pz Puhani, Im Blindfenster 7, ✆ 1770, III

Pz Schmidbauer, Osserstr. 5, ✆ 2805, II

Fw Schneider, Osterbachstr. 13, 1239, II

Fw Haslbeck, Straubinger Str. 8, ✆ 2365, II

Fw Monte Castello, Schlossberg 14, I

Kirchroth
Postal code: 94356; Area code: 09428

P Weiss-Hof, Regensburger Str. 40, ✆ 542, II

Kößnach
P Groß, Straubinger Str. 23, ✆ 094281574, III

Straubing
Postal code: 94315; Area code: 09421

🛈 Tourism office, Theresienpl. 2, ✆ 944307

H Theresientor, Theresienpl. 51, ✆ 8490, VI 📷

H Franziska, Regensburger Str. 42, ✆ 180480, V

H Villa, Bahnhofpl. 5b, ✆ 963670, V-VI

H Heimer, Schlesische Str. 131, ✆ 9810, IV-V 📷

H Seethaler, Theresienpl. 9, ✆ 93950, V-VI 📷

H Römerhof, Ittlinger Str. 136, ✆ 99820, V

H Gäubodenhof, Theresienpl. 32, ✆ 12275, IV 📷

H Röhrl, Theresienpl. 36, ✆ 430511, IV-V

H Wenisch, Innere Passauer Str. 59, ✆ 99310, V

H Bischofshof, Fraunhoferstr. 26, ✆ 12992, II 📷

H Zur Sonne, Landshuter Str. 113, ✆ 33235, III

H Asam, Wittelsbacherhöhe 1, ✆ 788680, VI

H Nothaft, Ittlinger Hauptstr. 3, ✆ 183390, V

Hg Schedlbauer, Landshuter Str. 78, ✆ 33838, III

Gh Landshuter Hof, Landshuter Str. 36, ✆ 30366, V 📷

Gh Reisinger, Sossauer Pl. 1, ✆ 10658, III

Gh Gabelsberger Hof, Gabelsberger Str. 21, ✆ 182113, III

P Weißes Rössl, Landshuter Str. 65, ✆ 96363366

BB Bredl, Steinweg 32, ✆ 184872 📷

🏠 Jugendherberge, Friedhofstr. 12, ✆ 80436, Open: 1.4-31.10, from 5 pm

⛺ Wundermühlweg 9, ✆ 89794, Open: May-Mid Oct.

Reibersdorf
Postal code: 94365; Area code: 09421

Gh Winklmeier, Richprechtstr. 15, ✆ 12295, II

Pz Schaller, Richprechtstr. 19, ✆ 10157, II

Bogen
Postal code: 94327; Area code: 09422

🛈 Tourist and Naturpark Info in the railway station, Bahnhofstr. 26, ✆ 808855

🛈 Cultural office, Stadtpl. 56, ✆ 505109

Gh Plötz, Großlintach 29, ✆ 1342, II

P Schreiber, Stadtpl. 23, ✆ 806993

H Zur Post, Stadtpl. 15, ✆ 1346, III

Gh Zur schönen Aussicht, Bogenberg 6, ✆ 1539, III

Breitenweinzier
Postal code: 94327; Area code: 09422

Pz Eberth, Breitenweinzier 1, ✆ 805373, II

Pfelling
Postal code: 94327; Area code: 09422

Gh Zum Donauufer, Pfelling 23, ✆ 2306, II 📷

Gh Pletl, Pfelling 13, ✆ 2178

Waltendorf
P ⛺ Plank-Hof, Waltendorf 19, ✆ 0171/3866335, III

Mariaposching
Postal code: 94553; Area code: 09906

P Killinger, Stadtfeldstr. 10a, ✆ 783, II

Gh Stöberl, Loham, Riedstr. 6, ✆ 201, II

Pz Elsner, Herzog-Odilo-Str. 13, ✆ 527

Kleinschwarzach
Postal code: 94560; Area code: 09906

⛺ & P Schreiber, Haus 1, ✆ 879

Metten
Postal code: 94526; Area code: 0991

🛈 Tourism office, Krankenhausstr. 22, ✆ 998050

H Hotel Gasthof Zum Kloster Metten, Neuhausener Str. 2, ✆ 9912101, IV

Gh Café am Kloster, Marktpl. 1, ✆ 9989380, III 📷

Pz Schreiber, Deggendorferstr. 29, ☎ 9959323, II

Deggendorf
Postal code: 94469; Area code: 0991
🅸 Tourist Information, Oberer Stadtpl. 1, ☎ 2960535
H Hotel-Gasthof Höttl, Luitpoldpl. 22, ☎ 3719960, V
H NH Parkhotel Deggendorf, Edlmairstr. 4, ☎ 34460, VI
H Donauhof, Hafenstr. 1, ☎ 38990, V
H Burgwirt, Deggendorfer Str. 7, ☎ 30045, IV
H Georgenhof, Altholzstr. 9, ☎ 4716, IV
H Anja, Altholzstr. 17, ☎ 8351, III-IV
H Stadthotel Deggendorf, Östl. Stadtgraben 13, ☎ 371640, V
H Landgasthof Zwickl, Schwarzacher Str. 3, ☎ 6306, III
P Haus Donaublick, Leoprechtstein 11, ☎ 5515, II
P Haus Ingeborg, Hans-Holbein-Str. 16, ☎ 25299, II
P Haus Gawlik, Regerstr. 5, ☎ 8791, II
P Müller, Ruselbergstr. 67, ☎ 21013, II
P Ring, Ruselbergstr. 64, ☎ 26991, II
🅰 Donaustrandhaus, Eginger Str. 42, ☎ 4324

Seebach
Area code: 09901
Gh Zwickl, Schwarzacher Str. 3, ☎ 6306, III

Niederalteich
Postal code: 94557; Area code: 09901
🅸 Town office, Gunterweg 3, ☎ 9353-0
P Zum Glück, Donaustr. 14a., ☎ 958992 o 0151/43246307, III
P Habereder, Uferstr. 13, ☎ 5657, II
Pz Mayrhofer, Odilostr. 5, ☎ 1265, II
P Nothaft, Mäuspoint 10, ☎ 6529, II

P Stattenberger, Gundelauer Str. 1, ☎ 5994, III

Osterhofen
Postal code: 94486; Area code: 09932
🅸 Tourist-Information, Stadtpl. 13, ☎ 403115
H Bayerischer Löwe, Vorstadt 10, ☎ 1497, V
H Pirkl, Altstadt 1, ☎ 1276, II
Gh Landgasthof Hötzl, Amsheimer Str. 10, ☎ 824, II

Rossfelden
🅰 Campingplatz Maier, Rossfelden 1, ☎ 2276

Winzer
Postal code: 94577; Area code: 09901
🅸 Tourist-Info, Schwanenkirchener Str. 2, ☎ 93570
Gh Zum grünen Baum, Passauer Str. 11, ☎ 7348, II
P Steinke, Bergstr. 6, ☎ 7270, III
P Biller, Ottach 1, ☎ 08545/8336, III
Fw Nirschl, Bachstr. 10, ☎ 948846, III
Fw Gruber, Aufeld 8, ☎ 900751, III

Neßlbach
Postal code: 94577; Area code: 08545
Gh Augenstein, Deggendorfer Str. 7, ☎ 341, III
Fw Kralitschek, Nelkenstr. 3, ☎ 8307, III

Hofkirchen
Postal code: 94544; Area code: 08545
🅸 Tourist-Information, Rathausstr. 1, ☎ 97180
Gh Buchner, Kaiserstr. 14, ☎ 911033, III
Gh Stanek, Zaundorf 4, ☎ 327, III
P Schiller, Fuggerweg 3, ☎ 1047
🅰 Ohetal, ☎ 515

Künzing
Postal code: 94550; Area code: 08549
Tourist-Information, Osterhofener Str. 2, ☎ 97310
Gh Thalhauser, Wallerdorf 7, ☎ 575 ◉
Pz Duschl, Girchinger Str. 4, ☎ 1227, II

Pleinting
Postal code: 94474; Area code: 08549
Gh Baumgartner, Hauptstr. 32, ☎ 910060, III
Gh Drei Mohren, Hauptstr. 36, ☎ 347, II

Vilshofen
Postal code: 94474; Area code: 08541
🅸 Tourist-Information, Stadtpl. 27, ☎ 208112
H Bairischer Hof, Vilsvorstadt 29, ☎ 5065, IV
Pz Sagerer, Alte Fischerg. 4, ☎ 7779, II ◉
H Wittelsbacher Zollhaus, Donaug. 10-12, ☎ 969600
H Landhof Eineder, Schönerting 42, ☎ 1323, III
Gh Gutsmidl, Böcklbacherstr 12, ☎ 5388, II
Gh Wolferstetter Bräu, Stadtpl. 14, ☎ 967935, III
Pz Flierl, Alte Feuerwehrg. 11, ☎ 1353, I

Windorf
Postal code: 94575; Area code: 08541
🅸 Touristinformation, Marktkpl. 23, ☎ 962640
H Zum Goldenen Anker, Marktpl. 42, ☎ 96650, II
Gh Fischerstüberl, Fischerstr. 21, ☎ 08546/624
P Donaublick, Nömerberg 20a, ☎ 967593 o. 0170/4332728, II ◉
P Moser, Marktpl. 40, ☎ 8275, II ◉

Gaishofen
Postal code: 94575; Area code: 08546

Gh Fischerstüberl, Fischerstr. 21, ☎ 624

Irring
Postal code: 94113; Area code: 08546
🅰 Dreiflüsse-Camping, Am Sonnenhang 8, ☎ 633

Passau
Postal code: 94032-36; Area code: 0851
🅸 Tourist-Information, Rathausplatz, ☎ 955980
🅸 Tourist-Information, Bahnhofstr. 28, ☎ 955980
H Cultellus, Kl. Messerg. 12, ☎ 49095204, V-VI ◉
Gh Goldenes Schiff, Unterer Sand 8, ☎ 34407, IV-V
H Weißer Hase, Heiliggeistg. 1, ☎ 92110, V-VII
H Innsento, Kapuzinerstr. 32, ☎ 38640-1, V-VII
H Rotel Inn, Donaulände, Nähe Hbf., ☎ 95160, IV ⚲
H Am Paulusbogen, Rindermarkt 2, ☎ 931060, V-VI
H Atrium, Neue Rieser Str. 6, ☎ 9886688, V-VII
H Dreiflüssehof, Danziger Str. 42/44, ☎ 72040, V-VI
H Schloss Ort, Im Ort 11, ☎ 34072, V-VII
H Altstadt-Hotel, Bräug. 23-29, ☎ 3370, V-VII
H StadtHotel, Gr. Klingerg. 17, ☎ 33069, IV-V
H IBB Hotel, Bahnhofstr. 29, ☎ 988300-0, VI-VII
H Burgwald, Salzweger Str. 9, ☎ 941690, V
H Achat Comfort, Neuburger Str. 79, ☎ 95180, V-VII
H Amedia Hotel Express, Neuburger Str. 128, ☎ 988420, IV-VI
Hg Wilder Mann, Am Rathausplatz, ☎ 35071, V-VI
Hg Passauer Wolf, Rindermarkt 6, ☎ 9315110, V-VII
Hg Herdegen, Bahnhofstr. 5, ☎ 955160, V-VI ◉
Hg Residenz, Fr.-Schäffer-Promenade, ☎ 989020, V-VII
Hg König, Untere Donaulände 1, ☎ 3850, V-VII
Hg Spitzberg, Neuburger Str. 29, ☎ 955480, V-VII

Hg Deutscher Kaiser, Bahnhofstr. 30, ✆ 9556615, V-VI
Gh Auer, Heininger Str. 26, ✆ 988990, V
Gh Rosencafé, Donaustr. 23 (Nordufer), ✆ 42811, III-V
Gh Zur Brücke, Landrichterstr. 13 (Ilzstadt-Hals),
    ✆ 43475, III
Gh Zur Triftsperre, Triftsperrstr. 15, ✆ 51162, III-V
Gh Blauer Bock, Höllg. 20, ✆ 34637, V
Gh Zum Streiblwirt, Rittsteiger Str. 87, ✆ 81382, III-IV
Gh Schäfer, Greppenweg/Neustift 3, ✆ 8516280, IV-V
P Vicus, Johann-Berglerstr. 2 ✆ 931050, V
P Fahrradpension Bäckerei Mandl, Bahnhofstr. 33,
    ✆ 34784, II
P Zur Goldenen Sonne, Unterer Sand 18, ✆ 2730, IV-V
P Rößner, Bräug. 19, ✆ 931350, IV
P Vilsmeier, Lindental 28a (Innstadt), ✆ 36313, III-IV
P Frickinger, Christdobl 13, ✆ 41222, IV
P Gambrinus, Haibach 20, ✆ 2905, IV
P Panorama, Angerstr. 59, ✆ 88199078, III, ohne Früh-
    stück
P Zur Freiheit, Wiener Str. 86, ✆ 4908491, III-IV
P Krinninger, Englmeierstr. 18, ✆ 41857
Pz Fiedler, Färberg. 5, ✆ 9890627, II
BB Fichtel, Halser Str. 27a, ✆ 9441594, III
Bh Hofbauerngut Sprödhuber, Hofbauerngut 1,
    ✆ 41263, IV
🏠 Jugendherberge Passau, Auf der Veste, Ober-
    haus 125, ✆ 493780 👁
⛺ Tent site Ilzstadt, Halser Str. 34, ✆ 41457

Kellberg
Postal code: 94136; Area code: 08501

ℹ️ Touristinformation Kellberg/Thyrnau, St.-Blasius-
    Str. 10, ✆ 320 o. 9117-30
Gh Kernmühle, Kernmühle 1, ✆ 567, II-III

Geographical Index

The *green numbers* indicate entries
in the accommodation guide.